JUDGING
THE WORLD COURT

A Twentieth Century Fund Paper

JUDGING THE WORLD COURT

BY THOMAS M. FRANCK

 Priority Press Publications / New York / 1986

The Twentieth Century Fund is an independent research foundation which undertakes policy studies of economic, political, and social institutions and issues. The Fund was founded in 1919 and endowed by Edward A. Filene.

Foreword

Americans are frequently described as being excessively litigious. If that is so, it follows that we regard the courts as the appropriate forum for resolving disputes. The earnest and frequently heated debates that usually take place over the selection of judges for both federal and state courts is another measure of the importance in which we hold the judiciary. We like to think that our concern and respect for the law is as evident internationally as it is domestically. We believe that the United States behaves properly in its relations with other countries, that it obeys the provisions of treaties to which it is a party, and that it is willing to accept the decisions of independent judges on issues in dispute.

The Reagan administration's withdrawal from the jurisdiction of the World Court as a result of the suit brought against the United States by Nicaragua made clear that our respect for international law is not all that it is proclaimed to be. Our withdrawal certainly did not provoke a strong domestic reaction. To be sure, the usual vocal critics of the administration voiced their dismay at this unilateral action. In general, though, Americans seemed to favor this show of independence, perhaps because of increasing dissatisfaction and resentment that the tides of world opinion have been running against us.

Both the Trustees and staff of the Twentieth Century Fund have been keenly interested in the evolving attitude of the U.S. government and its citizens toward international organizations. We are currently supporting and supervising a number of book-length projects dealing with various aspects of the subject—on the future of the United Nations, the problems of UNESCO, the changing nature of NATO, and the issue of multilateralism. Once the government and the World Court were in open conflict, we turned to Thomas M. Franck, director of the Center for International Studies at New York University School of Law, for an assessment of the troubled relationship. A recognized scholar of international law, he agreed to analyze the court, especially in its role in settling disputes involving the United States.

In the following pages, Franck provides a thoughtful and dispassionate account of the problem. He notes that our commitment to international law has always been somewhat suspect. That is partly because our feelings of national superiority and our desire to be independent—to the extent at times of reverting to isolationism—has usually led us to obey international law only when it suits our purposes. It also is because we do not give it the fealty we give to domestic lawmaking, which derives some of its legitimacy from its application to matters in which no political interest is at stake. International law, though, is essentially political, and the stakes tend to be high. Hence, we are chary of yielding our national sovereignty to others, especially when we fear that other countries may not yield theirs.

Yet the U.S. position in the Nicaraguan case does not—as many people seem to think—mean that we have renounced the World Court. We remain party to many treaties under which we continue to accept the court's jurisdiction. That being the case, Franck argues that the administration should do what it can to make our involvement consistent with its foreign policy objectives. He acknowledges that the United States will not—and should not—give up national sovereignty, but takes the view that in many circumstances our sovereignty can be advanced through international law and our adherence to the World Court's pronouncements.

We are grateful to Franck for his Fund Paper. It will, I am sure, inform and enhance the debate over the United States and the World Court.

M. J. Rossant, DIRECTOR
The Twentieth Century Fund
July 1986

Acknowledgments

I gratefully acknowledge support for this paper from the Twentieth Century Fund, as well as general support for my research from the Filomen D'Agostino and Max E. Greenberg Research Fund of New York University School of Law. In particular, I warmly acknowledge the gilt by association accruing from a series of critical legal interactions with Professor David W. Kennedy, while, in turn, fully absolving him of all guilt by association with the author's unredeemed views. My gratitude also extends to the Panel on the World Court of the American Society of International Law, funded by a Ford Foundation grant, from which I derived many useful ideas.

Thomas M. Franck
Professor of Law and Director
Center for International Studies
New York University School of Law.
Editor-in-Chief
The American Journal of International Law.

Contents

Preface

The potentially pivotal but vulnerable place occupied by the World Court in international relations is little known and less understood by most Americans. That it has intruded on the nation's consciousness at this time is due to two recent events. The first is the legal action—for, perhaps, as much as $400 million in damages—brought in 1984 by Nicaragua against the United States in connection with alleged activities conducted against the Sandinista regime based in Managua. The second is the related decision of the United States, in 1985 (effective as of April 7, 1986), to terminate its agreement to accept the compulsory jurisdiction of the World Court. These two events have compelled the president, the State Department, Congress, and the public, probably for the first time in forty years, to consider seriously the importance of the World Court—and, by extension, of international law—to the larger fabric of international relations and conflict management.

Whether to promote, and participate in, a world court has been discussed by Americans for a century—at times with great passion. That discussion is not over. For one thing, in a whole range of matters, the United States is still under the World Court's potential authority.

In the rhetoric of the World Court's American champions, the United States is a nation long and firmly wedded to the rule of law at home, and, thus, also in its foreign relations. The United States is a society morally committed to adjudication as a substitute for military force. It follows, *a fortiori*, that the United States must embrace, wholeheartedly, the idea of a world court. But were these assumptions ever true? Are they true now? Are they sensible? Is it realistic, in the face of continuing East-West and North-South animosities, to expect a superpower to subordinate its freedom of action to a tribunal of judges and a system of laws that are deliberately beyond national control? Is it prudent to do so if other major powers do not?

I would argue that the United States is, or ought to be, committed to the rule of law in some, but by no means all, of its interactions with other nations. To whatever extent the United States is willing to regulate its conduct by reference to international law, it should not be afraid to subject itself to litigation, at least not before a fair and reasonable tribunal. To the extent the nation's policy requires a free hand, such subordination is inconsistent, even dangerous.

The United States has now merely swung from acceptance of the World Court to rejection, from one polarity to another. Better calibration of its relation to the World Court—a realistic assessment of the requisites of its actual, present national interests and of the World Court's responsiveness to those interests—is needed. While a better calibrated approach will not yield a clear-cut answer to the question of whether the United States should support the World Court, it may, at least, provide a coherence between what the United States does and what it *says* it is doing.

Such coherence has been missing in U.S. relations with the World Court. The U.S. acceptance of the World Court's authority in 1946 was, essentially, a compromise between advocates of a "sovereign manifest destiny" and those of an "interdependent world order," achieved through verbal obfuscation of fundamental contradictions. In reality, the United States both accepted *and* rejected the jurisdiction of the World Court in 1946, in one misconceived effort at compromise between the internationalists and the unilateralists. This compromise resulted in the appearance of almost complete submission to the World Court superimposed on the reality of virtually no submission. A new policy must seek to reconcile these countervailing national tendencies. For just as there is no possibility today of a "sovereign" America, neither is there a viable system of universal, all-embracing interdependence.

The United States cannot both have a free hand and subordinate critical policy decisions to review by a panel of judges in The Hague. While it is impossible to have it both ways— despite decades of trying to do exactly that—it is not necessary to choose one alternative over the other. What is needed is a sober inventory that sorts out those areas of U.S. foreign relations that require unfettered self-determination from those that could benefit from impartial conflict resolution. The future of the U.S. relationship to the World Court lies with those activities carried on with a serious recognition of interdependence.

• 1 •

International Law and the World Court

International versus Domestic Law

The International Court of Justice, commonly known as the World Court, is housed in a palace—the Peace Palace—at The Hague, donated by an American philanthropist, Andrew Carnegie. Its labyrinthine halls, cavernous judges' chambers, and imposing courtroom make the World Court look like the Supreme Court of Mankind, which many of its founders intended it to be. Its judges wear somber robes of authority and listen to arguments by eminent counsel, much like their counterparts in the highest national courts. The disputes that come before them are about money, or violence, or contracts (treaties), or real estate (territory), much like those heard in national courts. But the litigants behind the lawyers are not doctors and patients, engineers and real estate operators, buyers and sellers. They are entire nations. And the law that the judges apply is not state or national, but international law.

International law is to international relations as drops of oil are to a bowl of water in which they have been immersed. The drops adhere to the surface of the water without becoming a part of it. If the water is calm, the drops tend to congeal into a seamless "skin" on the water's surface. But when the water is roiled, the drops tend to come apart, revealing large gaps.

When he was the Israeli foreign minister, Abba Eban once compared the United Nations (UN) to "an umbrella which is taken away the moment it starts raining." International law is vulnerable to the same charge; it is much admired by the states whose conduct it purports to regulate, but rarely heeded when there is an actual conflict between the law and a state's perceived self-interest.

In the domestic sphere, law is made by "the sovereign" (as, for example, by the Congress of the United States with the consent of the president), applied through courts in actual disputes,

3

and enforced by the police. International law, to some extent, is similar. While there is no global "sovereign," the "citizenry" of the international community—that is, the states—enact international law by negotiating, signing, and ratifying treaties. Some of these treaties—for example, the UN Charter—are of virtually universal adherence, while others are law for the smaller number of states that have chosen to join in ratification.

In U.S. law, the "sovereign will" also may be found in the habitual conduct of citizens—a source of law known as "customary" or "common." So, too, in the international community, the rules by which states habitually regulate their conduct is recognized as customary law and these create the expectation that what is usually done ought to, and will, be done. Much of the law traditionally applied to navigation on the high seas and in coastal waters—both in time of peace and war—while now codified in treaties, developed first as "custom." Somewhat as article 6 of the U.S. Constitution declares treaties part of the "supreme Law of the Land," so the courts of the United States have held that such international "customary" law is part of the law of the United States.[1]

Just as the U.S. legal system is equipped with courts, the UN Charter, in article 92, established the World Court as "the principal judicial organ of the United Nations." It makes all members of the United Nations "*ipso facto* parties to the Statute of the International Court of Justice," which is appended to, and "forms an integral part" of the charter.[2]

The World Court traces its origins to the Permanent Court of International Justice, which occupied a somewhat analogous position in the arrangement established by the Covenant of the League of Nations, and, more remotely, to the Permanent Court of Arbitration established at the end of the nineteenth century on the initiative of Czar Nicholas II. In addition, the international community answers to various regional, specialized, and ad hoc tribunals that have jurisdiction over fewer states and serve more limited or specialized purposes. These include the European and Inter-American courts of human rights, the court of the European Community, and, in the future when it comes into being, the Law of the Sea tribunal.

While there is no police force in the international system to compel recourse to judicial settlement or to enforce the decisions of judges, the UN Charter does require all members to settle their disputes by "negotiation, enquiry, mediation, conciliation, arbitration, judicial settlement, resort to regional agencies or arrangements, or other peaceful means of their own choice."[3] The

UN Charter empowers the Security Council to recommend the appropriate procedure for settlement in each dispute, taking "into consideration that legal disputes should as a general rule be referred by the parties to the International Court of Justice. . . ."[4] The charter further obliges each UN member "to comply with the decision of the International Court of Justice in any case to which it is a party"[5] and stipulates that if a state fails to carry out a decision, then the Security Council "may . . . decide upon measures to be taken to give effect to the judgment."[6] Violators of international law do not always get away with illegal conduct, as the governments of Rhodesia and South Africa found out when sanctions were imposed—with some success—by the Security Council.

While the international community may thus be said to be equipped with the necessary components of a legal regime—"sovereign" sources, judiciaries, and a police power—these are, at best, pale clones of the law-making institutions of the national communities. Although broadly accepted treaties facilitate diverse global activities—from the delivery of mail to transmission of radio signals, to fishing, to space travel—large areas remain underregulated or in a "state of nature," with each nation doing pretty much as it pleases. For example, it is not clear whether states issuing mining permits to companies to extract mineral deposits from the deep seabed beneath the high seas—in defiance of a drafted, but as yet unimplemented, treaty declaring those resources the "common heritage of mankind"—are acting lawfully or unlawfully.

As for the police power, while the Security Council has, on one occasion, sent two disputant states—Britain and Albania—to the World Court,[7] there have been no instances in which it ordered a recalcitrant litigant to obey a court order. Nor is it clear whether a state that has won an award in the World Court can enforce it in the domestic courts of states where the loser has assets. Further, while in the past almost all decisions of the World Court were obeyed voluntarily, in recent years more and more states—France, Iceland, Iran, and, most recently, the United States—have become selective about deferring to the World Court's opinions.

The Powers that Be

Article 2 of the Statute of the International Court of Justice provides: "The Court shall be composed of a body of independent judges, elected regardless of their nationality from among persons of high moral character, who possess the qualifications required in their respective countries for appointment to the highest judicial offices, or are jurisconsults of recognized competence in international law." Stipulating that the World Court shall consist of fifteen persons meeting those qualifications, article 3 adds that "no two. . .may be nationals of the same State. . . ." Article 9 makes this "geographical distribution" even more explicit in cautioning "the electors" to see to it that the bench as a whole is representative "of the main forms of civilization and of the principal legal systems of the world." The statute stipulates no lower or upper age limit for World Court judges.

The nomination and election of judges proceeds by a somewhat arcane procedure. Shabtai Rosenne, in his definitive work on the law and practice of the World Court,[8] has shrewdly observed that the political nature of this process should not be surprising to those who understand that judicial selection in the national systems of virtually every nation is inevitably political, since the alternative would be an even more unsatisfactory arrangement by which new judges are selected by other sitting judges or by a judicial service commission—procedures that are too elitist for the tastes of most publics.

Articles 4 and 5 of the Statute of the International Court of Justice provide that candidates be nominated through "national groups." These are nominating colleges of up to four persons, chosen by the respective governments, serving for six years with the possibility of reappointment. Each "national group" may nominate up to four persons for each judicial vacancy, not more than two being of the group's own nationality.[9]

The purpose of this, evidently, is to make the role of governments appear somewhat less intrusive. In fact, at least as far as the United States is concerned, that appearance is not wholly misleading. When President Jimmy Carter tried to offer the U.S. seat on the World Court to former Supreme Court Justice Arthur Goldberg, he was prevented from doing so by the national group's preference for Richard R. Baxter of the Harvard Law School.[10] The process also mildly encourages judicial independence. The Polish judge on the World Court, for example, in his most recent reelection bid, was nominated not only by his own country but also by various non-Communist national groups, including that of the United States.

Unlike the system of nominations, the process of election is openly political. The Statute of the International Court of Justice provides that a candidate is elected on obtaining a majority in both the UN General Assembly and Security Council.[11] Because terms are staggered to maintain continuity, five of the fifteen judgeships are up for election or reelection every three years. Balloting continues in the two UN chambers until all vacancies have been filled.[12]

In recent years, this electoral process has come under increasing criticism. Critics assert that the elections have become unseemly, as candidates have begun to campaign openly in the United Nation's halls and as elections to the World Court have become comingled, in the political organs of the United Nations, with elections for vacancies in various other organs, committees, and specialized agencies. The result, it is alleged, has been a form of political horse-trading that does not promote the selection of the most highly qualified candidates.

While there is nothing in the Statute of the International Court of Justice to ensure the election of judges from the "Big Five" states that occupy permanent seats in the Security Council (Britain, China, France, the United States, and the Soviet Union), and their veto does not apply to balloting for judges, their candidates usually have been elected—except in the case of China during the height of the conflict between the Communist and Nationalist regimes. But such a result is not inevitable; in 1945, the permanent members accounted for five of eleven seats in the Security Council, but since the 1963 enlargement, their role has been diluted to only five of fifteen.[13]

While the process of electing judges is political, the Statute of the International Court of Justice seeks to guarantee the independence of a judge, once elected, by a nine-year tenure.[14] All members are eligible for reelection and, even if not reelected, serve on the World Court until the conclusion of the proceedings in a case before them.[15] Every three years the judges elect a president from among their number. As it hears cases, the World Court ordinarily sits with all judges on the bench. With the agreement of the parties, however, the World Court may also constitute chambers of three or more, a practice recently used in a case between Canada and the United States.[16]

The Statute of the International Court of Justice does not require the judge of a state that is a party to a case to step down while it is being heard. If he or she does not do so, however, the other party is entitled to name an ad hoc judge.[17] If neither litigant has a judge on the bench, each may make an ad hoc appointment. This procedure introduces a whiff of arbitration into what is otherwise a judicial proceeding. However, in every case so far, the balance of power has been firmly with the preponderance of judges who are nationals of neither party.

Who Uses the World Court?

Article 34 of the Statute of the International Court of Justice limits access to "states," thereby denying it to individuals, corporations, and, even, international organizations (except for an "advisory" opinion). States seeking to litigate need not be members of the United Nations, as long as they have accepted the World Court's jurisdiction in general, or for a particular case.

It is, therefore, relatively easy for any states wishing to go before the World Court to do so. But states are under no obligation to use the World Court in any particular dispute unless: (1) they have specially accepted the general compulsory jurisdiction of the World Court in accordance with article 36(2) of its statute, or (2) they have entered into an agreement with the other disputant to refer that one dispute to the World Court, or (3) the dispute arises under article 36(1) of the statute, which is to say that they are parties to a treaty or international agreement stipulating that disputes between the parties to the agreement—usually over the interpretation of the text—are to be referred to the World Court. The distinction between 36(2) and 36(1) jurisdiction is important. States that have accepted compulsory jurisdiction under article 36(2) can be taken to the World Court by any other state, in any legal dispute—although only to the extent that this other state has accepted the same obligation.[18] Under article 36(1), however, only parties to a treaty can take each other to court—and only in disputes arising out of that treaty. This suggests that article 36(1) is a much narrower basis for jurisdiction than article 36(2).

Article 36(2) jurisdiction is both "compulsory" and "voluntary" in the sense that a state accepts the compulsory jurisdiction of the World Court by a special agreement and can terminate that agreement on its own initiative when it wishes, as the United States has demonstrated. By contrast, adherence to article 36(1) is not terminable except by terminating the specific treaty obligation.

There are additional bases for the World Court's jurisdiction. It may be asked by the General Assembly or the Security Council to give an advisory opinion on any legal question related to a subject before the United Nations. Article 96 of the UN Charter also states that other "organs of the United Nations and specialized agencies, which may at any time be so authorized by the General Assembly, may also request advisory opinions of the Court on legal questions arising within the scope of their activities." The U.S. member of the World Court, Judge Stephen Schwebel, has recently recommended that the secretary-general of the United Nations be empowered to request advisory opinions on his own authority.

If an authorized organ seeks the advice of the World Court, the matter normally cannot be kept from the court, despite the opposition of any particular state. In practice, therefore, some disputes have been heard under circumstances in which one or more of the disputants might not otherwise have agreed to adjudicate. Thus, seeking advice becomes, in effect, a "backdoor" route to the World Court. Still, an "advisory opinion" is precisely that—advisory. As such, it does not bind. The requesting organ, however, may adopt the advice by resolution, in which case it becomes binding—but only on that body.

Some states whose interests have been adversely affected by advisory opinions—France, the Soviet Union, and Morocco[19] —have simply ignored them. When that happens, the states whose interests the World Court has vindicated criticize the "futility" of going to the trouble of using a court whose opinions are not enforced, while those that have lost attack the judges for being politicized and overreaching the proper limits of their fiat.

The Caseload

For two decades from the mid-1950s, the World Court sat largely idle and was roundly criticized for being an irrelevant sinecure. In the next decade, business began to pick up, in part because it was actively solicited by the judges, who traveled to the UN General Assembly and to leading national capitals in search of disputes and clients. As a result, the World Court was criticized for engaging in the global equivalent of ambulance chasing. When the World Court has labored long years (at great financial cost) to resolve relatively minor disputes—such as the disposition of a Belgian-Canadian electricity franchise in Barcelona—it is characterized as a trivial pursuit. When, on the other hand, it seeks to determine the legal right of the United States to engage in a covert war with Nicaragua, it is condemned (by Washington) for trespassing into the sacrosanct precincts of politics.

In its forty years of existence, the World Court has taken some 115 decisions in contentious cases and advisory proceedings. Since the World Court's activities in a dispute are divided into various "phases"—preliminary, jurisdictional, and on the merits—and many orders of the World Court are essentially procedural, the number of decisions and orders far exceeds the actual number of disputes adjudicated. Nevertheless, this record is not insubstantial.

The World Court has handled numerous disputes over title to territory (border towns between Holland and Belgium; islands in the English Channel; enclaves or splinters of land on the Swiss-French border, on the Thai-Cambodian boundary, and in West Africa). It has dealt with disputes over the waters of rivers and over the resources on the ocean floor and in fishing grounds off Norway, Iceland, and Maine. It has ruled on property matters as disparate as a whole country (Namibia and the Spanish Sahara) and the rights of individual aliens. It has considered the duties of a state toward foreign enterprises conducting business on its territory and those of a UN senior official running a peacekeeping operation in the Middle East. It has handled cases dealing with ships on public waters that were blown up by mines, and diplomats who were taken hostage. Its opinions have been sought as to whether French nuclear testing in the Pacific violates the environmental rights of Australia and New Zealand, and whether UN members are legally bound to pay the annual assessments fixed by the General Assembly when they disagree with an activity for which they are used.

That record evokes further differences between the domestic and the international legal systems. What makes the role of the courts in the United States, or any other country, feasible is not merely the existence of sovereign-made laws and the enforcement power of the police, but also the benevolent indifference to judicial decisions on the part of most of those with power in the society. The government, the Congress, and most public and special interest groups simply do not care how most cases turn out, as long as they are resolved. The vast preponderance of cases brought before courts in the United States involve no ascertainable public interest other than that the dispute be peacefully and expeditiously terminated by judicial pronouncement.

By handling these "little disputes" efficiently, the courts earn gratitude and build up a reservoir of credit that can be drawn upon when the judges are propelled into cases that do engage grand public passions. What enables the Supreme Court of the United States to decide a landmark desegregation case like *Brown v. Board of Education* is the aura of its institutional indispensability earned in myriad "little" decisions. It is not simply, or even primarily, police enforcement that makes possible domestic adjudication, it is the weight of public opinion in favor of the *process* and its indifference to any particular outcome.

The World Court, almost by definition, operates in a context largely bereft of "little" cases. While the subject matter of most cases is not of the cataclysmic war/peace variety, every case pits one state against another. There is no dispute before the World Court that does not engage adversarial state interest. Thus even "little" cases are important because they come before the World Court as disputes between the leviathans—between totalitarian and democratic, socialist and free market, developed and underdeveloped states. And, paradoxically, the World Court, while operating in such a charged political environment, must constantly confront the exaggerated expectation that judges will replace armies in resolving the world's conflicts.

• 2 •

A Brief History

A Global Vision

When, on January 18, 1985, the United States announced that it would no longer participate in the litigation brought against it by Nicaragua, and, on October 7, notified the World Court of its intent to terminate, after six months, its acceptance of the court's mandatory jurisdiction under article 36(2), Washington appeared to be turning its back on two centuries of American leadership in the cause of world peace through law and courts. This appearance, however, is misleading. True, American leaders have long emphasized the U.S. commitment to a world order of laws and judges. But that rhetoric has been, at best, only dimly manifest in the nation's conduct.

Admittedly, the idea of a world court did originate primarily in the American imagination during the nineteenth and early twentieth centuries. Secretary of State John Hay was not misrepresenting when, in 1899, he referred to the "long-continued and widespread interest among the people of the United States in the establishment of an international court."[1] But that is only a part of the story that must be understood if we are to make sensible policy choices for the future.

The beginning of the modern era of third-party dispute settlement dates from November 19, 1794, when American Secretary of State John Jay signed the famous treaty with Britain bearing his name.[2] It established three boards of arbitration to resolve disputes ranging from the Saint Croix River boundary to citizens' debt and property claims. In each case, the arbitration successfully resolved the dispute and, where appropriate, fixed responsibility and assessed damages. Thereby, it became a model of civilized settlement of disputes by the application of principled reasoning.

The next major landmark was the signing, in 1871, of the Treaty of Washington establishing four arbitrations dealing with the conduct of Britain during the American Civil War.[3] The most famous of these became known as the "Alabama" claims, so-called after the British-built vessel with which Confederate forces, using British colonial ports, had raided Union ships and cargoes. Once again, successful arbitration relieved both nations of what had become a menacing escalation in popular passions.

The Alabama arbitration took place in Geneva, Switzerland, before a five-member board consisting of three "neutral" judges and one each from the United States and Britain. The neutrals were named by the president of the Swiss Confederation, the king of Italy, and the emperor of Brazil. Over the sole dissent of the British arbitrator, the tribunal awarded $15.5 million to the United States for Britain's failure to carry out its obligation of neutrality. The *New York Times* hailed the result as one to be "rejoiced over by every man who is anxious for the advance of peace, and especially by every reasonable American."[4] The *Times* stated that the proceeding had demonstrated decisively that national conduct must have "regard to international law."[5]

The impetus toward peace through law and tribunals that came to feature so prominently in American public rhetoric during this period cannot be attributed solely to outcomes favorable to the United States. Deeper roots of the idea of systematic recourse to law and judges—an idea firmly rooted in the American national experience—revealed themselves in the statement by President Benjamin Harrison to the First Pan-American Conference of 1889-90, which had drafted a hemispheric arbitration agreement. "We rejoice," he said, "that you have found in the organization of our Government something suggestive and worthy of imitation."[6]

Harrison's sentiment was echoed repeatedly during the next ninety years by American leaders who proclaimed that a world of international law and international tribunals would be a natural, even historically inevitable, extrapolation of a good American idea. The American federal system had proven the importance of courts as umpires between the states, and between the states and the federal authorities. The idea was ripe for global adoption.

From the very beginning, however, this optimistic global vision encountered trouble. Not a single nation—including the United States—ratified the hemispheric treaty lauded by Harrison. Nevertheless, during the same decade, successful arbitrations were carried on between the United States and Britain regarding fur seals, the Venezuela-British Guiana boundary, and, a few years later, the Alaskan panhandle.

Efforts to institutionalize these occasional processes continued to founder, however. In 1896, President Grover Cleveland transmitted to the Senate the most ambitious U.S. commitment so far to systematic arbitration. The Olney-Pauncefote treaty, the president noted, would ensure "the arbitration of all matters in difference between the United States and Britain" and thus "not only makes war between the parties to it a remote possibility, but precludes those fears and rumors of war which of themselves too often assume the proportions of national disaster."[7] The *New York Times* greeted the treaty with a five-column editorial, praising "an instrument that will pass into history with the Magna Carta in England and Declaration of Independence in the United States."[8] It continued that "in the course of time the method here suggested for the settlement of disputes will so commend itself to the peoples now burdened by great standing armies that their rulers will be constrained by the sentiment of the masses to adopt it" for all disputes everywhere.[9]

Succeeding Cleveland, President William J. McKinley, in his 1897 inaugural address, hailed the treaty and proudly reminded the American public that it was "clearly the result of our own initiative since it has been recognized as the leading feature of our foreign policy throughout our entire national history—the adjustment of difficulties by judicial methods rather than force of arms—and since it presents to the world the glorious example of reason and peace, not passion and war, controlling relations between two of the great nations of the world, an example certain to be followed by others. . . ."[10]

The Senate debated Olney-Pauncefote from February to May 1897. Objections focused on the "failure" to reserve matters of national honor, territorial integrity, domestic policy, and claims against states of the union. Senators also objected to the fact that they would not be called upon to approve the submitting of each case before it could go to arbitration. These "shortcomings" were remedied by numerous amendments that made the original draft unrecognizable. Even so, on May 5, the treaty failed to secure the requisite two-thirds Senate majority.[11]

The minority report of the Senate Foreign Relations Committee provided the rationale for this defeat. Treaties, it stated, "seem made to be broken, as fortresses are said to be made to be taken; and it is questionable after all whether an open field and the chance of a fair fight are not the best protection to a peace-loving nation, both in war and diplomacy. . . ."[12] Without an "unqualified right of appeal to arms no nation can be independent."[13]

The battle over ratification of the Olney-Pauncefote treaty drew clearly the lines between the incompatible unilateralist and multilateralist strains in American foreign relations. That configuration has changed little in the succeeding nine decades. The multilateralists then, and up to the beginning of the 1980s, controlled the executive branch. They spoke for the nation through the White House, State Department, and eastern and southeastern establishment. And they probably had the support of a soft, narrow majority in Congress. Yet, a vocal and large congressional minority and a blocking third in the Senate continued to fear and oppose that loss of sovereignty that they perceived to be the inevitable—and excessive—cost of submission to international adjudication. The internationalists got all the attention but it was the unilateralists who usually had the last say.

The Continuing Struggle

The multilateralist vision was fulsomely expressed by U.S. Supreme Court Justice David J. Brewer at the 1895 annual meeting of the American Bar Association. "There will never be one great parliament, one Federal republic embracing all races and ruling the world. . ." he said, "but the lawyer will work out the final peace. . . .The world is becoming familiar with the international arbitrations, and the settlement of disputes thereby; and every successful arbitration is but a harbinger of the day when all disputes between nations shall be settled in courts of peace and not by the roar of cannon and waste of blood."[14]

At a special meeting on April 16, 1896, the State Bar Association of New York petitioned President Cleveland to work toward creating a permanent world tribunal, because "it is quite within the possibility of the educated intellects of the leading powers of the world to agree upon a plan for a great central world's court that, by the common consent of nations, shall eventually have jurisdiction of all disputes arising between Independent Powers that cannot be adjusted by friendly diplomatic negotiations."[15]

Such rhetoric represented nothing like a national consensus. It emanated from a loose coalition of influential groups—primarily leading eastern and southern lawyers, Quaker pacifists, mainstream Protestant clergy and laity, and several preeminent journals. Their views received a respectful, even sympathetic, hearing in the White House. The Department of State was disproportionately populated, at the top, by their adherents. A majority of Congress probably agreed, more or less. But they were

never—then, or in the next century—able to translate that vision into a winning political cause, nor did the nation ever
seriously contemplate investing any significant share of national
sovereignty in its realization.

Instead, there was a continuing struggle between the
multilateralists and the unilateralists, with the former arguing
for the exportability, indeed the universal applicability, of various
unique features of American constitutionalism. They emphasized the salutary way that the umpiring role, acquired by U.S.
courts in the first decades after the ratification of the Constitution, had facilitated peaceful settlement of disputes that most
other societies resolved with ballots or guns. The nationalists,
on the other hand, argued that the United States, protected by
two oceans and an increasingly powerful military, and endowed with a tradition of fair play and non-self-aggrandizement
in international relations, had little reason to subordinate its national self-reliance to an untried juridical compact with less for-
tunate or more venal nations.

For almost a century there has been confusion about the outcome of this conflict, in part because neither side was ever willing to concede defeat, but also because of a growing gap between
what the multilateralists professed and what they were able to
accomplish. They tended to speak, but could not act, for the
nation; and they continued to sound as if they were winning
even as they lost encounter after encounter on the domestic front.

The Permanent Court of Arbitration

As the nineteenth century drew to a close, the multilateralists
once again went on the initiative, seeking to establish a world
court at a series of conferences convened by the Russian czar
at The Hague.[16] At the first of these, in 1899, Secretary of State
Hay instructed the U.S. delegation to go beyond the czar's limited
proposal and attempt to secure agreement on a full-scale world
tribunal with very wide powers.[17] The U.S. initiative proved
premature. The conference settled for a much less dramatic
British-Russian proposal, a blueprint for a permanent court of
arbitration that was neither a court nor permanent, but, rather,
a list of distinguished jurists from which disputing nations, by
entering into case-by-case agreement, might choose a panel to
hear a particular dispute.[18] The result was a legal fiction, a device
that philosopher Jeremy Bentham characterized as a "lie of the
worst sort."[19]

Nevertheless, the administration of Theodore Roosevelt set out to negotiate a series of bilateral treaties that would oblige the parties to use the Permanent Court of Arbitration in all legal disputes. Twenty-seven were signed in all, including agreements with Britain, France, Switzerland, Germany, Portugal, Italy, Spain, Austria-Hungary, Mexico, Sweden-Norway, and Japan.[20] The Senate, in each instance, promptly replaced the mandatory submission provisions with a requirement for special agreements subject to prior senatorial consent, whereupon Roosevelt angrily withdrew them from consideration. He wrote the Senate, "it is mere nonsense to have a treaty which does nothing but say . . . that whenever we choose there shall be another arbitration treaty. . . . Now as far as I am concerned, I wish either to take part in something that means something or else not to have any part in it at all."[21]

At the second conference convened at The Hague, in 1907, Secretary Elihu Root instructed the U.S. delegation again to press for a real judiciary "which would pass upon questions between nations with the same impartial and impersonal judgment that the Supreme Court of the United States gives to questions arising between citizens of the different States." If such a court were established, he said, "there can be no doubt that nations would be much more ready to submit their controversies to its decision than they are now to take the chances of arbitration."[22] The results, once again, were minimal.

With that, the United States renewed its efforts to develop a network of broad bilateral agreements. In the summer of 1911, Secretary of State Philander C. Knox signed treaties with France and Britain in which the parties agreed to submit all "differences hereafter arising. . .which are judiciable in their nature. . . ."[23] The Senate Foreign Relations Committee criticized the treaties as "very large and general"[24] and, under the leadership of Lodge, added and deleted freely from the agreed text. Arbitrations were not to touch on questions of "purely governmental policy," including immigration, admission of aliens to schools, or matters affecting territorial integrity.[25] A disgruntled President William H. Taft withdrew the mutilated instruments.

The Permanent Court of International Justice

Thereafter, Europe and the United States became otherwise engaged. As World War I drew to a close, however, the search for international peace through law and tribunals resumed.

Although the United States failed to join the League of Nations, even some of the leading opponents of that organization— President Warren G. Harding, Elihu Root, and John Bassett Moore—favored membership in the Permanent Court of International Justice, which had also been established at the Versailles Peace Conference. Although states joining the court did not thereby accept its compulsory jurisdiction, members could voluntarily agree to an "optional clause" that would have that effect.[26]

The United States never contemplated accepting the "optional clause" but, for almost twenty years, did debate whether to join. After the defeat of the Treaty of Versailles, Harding's secretary of state, Charles Evans Hughes, stated: "We favor, and have always favored, an international court of justice for the determination according to judicial standards of judiciable international disputes. . . ."[27] The White House then announced that, after completing negotiations to obtain a voice in the process of nominating and electing judges, it planned to recommend approval of the court's protocol.[28] This solution continued to be favored by Presidents Calvin Coolidge, Herbert Hoover, and Franklin D. Roosevelt. Yet it never captured the support of the two-thirds of the Senate needed to ratify the various agreements worked out with the court.

In seeking to convince the Senate's unilateralists, Coolidge described the Permanent Court of International Justice as "a convenient instrument to which we could go, but to which we could not be brought."[29] In choosing this tactic, Coolidge helped to foster the illusion that effective participation in a world court can be had without some meaningful derogation from national sovereignty. Hoover, in 1930, argued that we would be joining an important "effort of the nations to establish a great agency," while at the same time reassuring that it would have no real power, that "we cannot be summoned before this Court."[30] In 1935, Roosevelt, urging ratification, assured the senators that the "sovereignty of the United States will be in no way diminished or jeopardized by such action."[31] They responded on January 29 by voting for the proposal 52 to 36, seven votes short of the required two-thirds majority.[32]

That ended the campaign for the Permanent Court of International Justice. The unilateralist position was summed up by Senator Park Trammell of Florida, who said: "I am not willing to vote to have the United States enter this Court and go into a trial before judges representing nations which, generally speaking, are unsympathetic to America. . . ."[33] Senator Huey B. Long of Louisiana, less delicately, declared that "we are being rushed in pell-mell to get into this World Court so that Senor Ab Jap or some other something from Japan can pass upon our controversies."[34]

The International Court of Justice

The surge of U.S. internationalism that followed World War II carried along many former isolationists and nationalists, including such prominent leaders as Senator Arthur H. Vandenberg and Robert A. Taft. In 1945, America seemed on the verge of decisive commitment to the multilateralist vision.

As early as July 1942, Secretary of State Cordell Hull had called for the creation of a new international court of justice to settle disputes by peaceful means.[35] Within the State Department, a small task force began to draft the constitution for a successor to the Permanent Court of International Justice.[36] By mid-1944, President Roosevelt had endorsed its plans, and one month later, the U.S. government handed its Soviet, British, and Chinese counterparts a "Tentative Proposal for a General International Organization" that included a draft provision for a world tribunal.[37]

Agreement was quickly reached in principle. On October 9, 1944, the Big Four recorded their consensus in favor of "an international court of justice which should constitute the principal judicial organ of the Organization."[38] Only two weeks before the San Francisco conference, in April 1945, a committee of jurists met to draw up the final plans. Secretary of State Edward R. Stettinius told the delegates that it was "scarcely possible to envisage the establishment of an International Organization for the maintenance of peace without having as a component part thereof a truly international judicial body."[39] Salient among the issues still to be resolved, however, was the old question of compulsory jurisdiction. Should membership in the new UN organization also entail an obligation to adjudicate legal disputes, or should the new court's jurisdiction, like that of its predecessor, be essentially voluntary? This time around, a large majority of the participants favored some form of real compulsory jurisdiction applicable to all.[40]

The two most powerful participants, however—the Soviet Union and the United States—emphatically disagreed. President

Harry S. Truman's initial instinct had been to side with the smaller nations' demand, reasoning that if "we were going to have a court it ought to be a court that would work, with compulsory jurisdiction."[41] Before the showdown, however, he was converted to a more cautious strategy, primarily to prevent the main issue—membership in the UN—from being freighted with the additional issue of compulsory jurisdiction. Moscow's delegate made it clear that his government would not join if its wishes in this respect were disregarded. Green H. Hackworth, the legal adviser to the State Department, confirmed that "some States would find it difficult to become a party" to the UN Charter if they thereby were required to submit to the court. He predicted, however, that the United States, "at an early date," would submit voluntarily to compulsory jurisdiction under an optional protocol.[42]

In a "spirit of reconciliation" the majority gave way.[43] In the words of a British delegate, holding out for the "ideal would only impair the possibility of obtaining general accord."[44] On June 25, the UN Charter was unanimously adopted, with the Statute of the International Court of Justice an integral part—thereby avoiding the need for separate ratification. While this ensured that all members of the UN would also adhere to the International Court of Justice (the World Court), that adherence was little more than another legal fiction, at least until such time as each state took the additional step of adopting the optional clause, now known as article 36(2) of the statute.

The U.S. Senate approved the UN Charter and Statute of the International Court of Justice by a vote of 89 to 2 and the president promptly notified ratification on June 26, 1945.[45]

On the very day the Senate approved the UN Charter, Senator Wayne L. Morse of Oregon introduced a draft resolution calling for accepting the compulsory jurisdiction of the new court. Senate Foreign Relations Committee hearings began in July 1946. All witnesses testified in favor of submission, including Undersecretary of State Dean Acheson, who reasoned that the "record of the United States in its international dealings is such that it should not dread to have its acts reviewed by a court of law."[46] But by mid-1946, the cold war had begun and the climate was quite different from a year earlier.

Nevertheless, a foreign relations subcommittee concluded that acceptance of compulsory jurisdiction would reflect "relative unanimity of American public opinion" and the full committee unanimously recommended favorable action. It warned that if "individual members can refuse to be hailed into Court, a regime of law in the international community will never be realized." Calling on the nation to set a good example, it held out the promise that a favorable Senate vote would "develop a spirit of trust and confidence, particularly on the part of the small states, towards the United States."[47]

It soon became apparent that the momentum that had carried the United States into the UN had abated. Vandenberg moved to exclude from the World Court's compulsory jurisdiction those disputes that might arise under a multilateral treaty to which the United States is a party unless all the affected parties to the treaty were also parties to the litigation, or unless the United States specifically agreed to be sued despite the absence of some of these potential parties.[48] But it was the Foreign Relations Committee chair, Senator Connally, who sounded once more the briefly muted nationalist tocsin. "I am in favor of the United Nations," he said, "but I am also for the United States of America. I do not want to surrender the sovereignty or the prestige of the United States . . . because the best hope of the world lies in the survival of the United States with its concepts of democracy, liberty, freedom, and advancement under its institutions."[49] Connally moved an amendment to exclude from the World Court's compulsory jurisdiction all "domestic" matters *as determined by the United States of America.*[50] Senator Morse replied that the amendment was, in reality, "a political veto on questions of a judicial character," which would "be instantly recognized as such by all the other countries."[51] He warned that other states would follow our bad example, creating a boomerang effect.

But once again the multilateralists compromised. "There isn't a single nose that wasn't counted," Senator Thomas reported.[52] The Senate adopted the Connally reservation by a vote of 51 to 12 with thirty-three senators not voting and, on August 2, approved the amended advice and consent resolution by a vote of 60 to 2 with thirty-four senators not voting.[53]

In presenting the American accession to the UN secretary-general on August 26, acting U.S. Representative Herschel V. Johnson stated that it demonstrated U.S. commitment "to a great development of the rule of law in international relations through a broad acceptance of the function of the Court in the spirit of the Charter."[54] That remark recalled the shrewd observation made in 1928 by Manley O. Hudson, that the government of the United States "seldom loses an opportunity to profess its loyalty to international arbitration in the abstract. . .the expression of this sentiment has become so conventional that a popular impression prevails that it accords with the actual policy of the United States."[55]

Unilateralism Returns

For thirty-five years following this largely illusory acceptance of the World Court's compulsory jurisdiction, presidents—both Republican and Democratic—continued to press for repeal of the Connally reservation. Speaking at the University of New Delhi, in India, President Dwight D. Eisenhower renewed the call for universal compulsory jurisdiction. "It is better to lose a point now and then in an international tribunal," he said, "and gain a world in which everyone lives at peace under the rule of law."[56] His attorney general, William D. Rogers, speaking at New York University, said: "The time has come, I think, to reexamine the domestic jurisdiction reservation. . . .The International Court needs more support if it is to succeed. . . ."[57] Meanwhile, the U.S. government was brandishing the Connally reservation as a shield to prevent the World Court from taking jurisdiction over a suit brought against the United States by Switzerland concerning the wartime seizure of commercial assets.[58]

The efforts to repeal the Connally reservation finally succeeded, but not in the way Eisenhower had envisaged. Only when the United States threw out the baby did it get rid of the bathwater. In April 1984, after learning that Nicaragua was about to file suit against the United States, the State Department notified the World Court that it was altering American acceptance of compulsory jurisdiction, with immediate effect, to exclude "disputes with any Central American state."[59] In 1946, the Senate had added a requirement of six-months' notice for termination precisely so the world would see that the United States would never run away from a law suit. In 1984, the United States made the argument—among others—that the notice requirement did not apply because mere "alteration" is different from "termination." In November 1984, the World Court overwhelmingly rejected that argument and took jurisdiction. The Reagan administration, thereafter, announced that it would no longer participate in the case.

Explaining this decision, the United States asserted that the Central American conflict was "not a narrow legal dispute" but an "inherently political problem that is not appropriate for judicial resolution," and added that when "the United States accepted the Court's compulsory jurisdiction in 1946, it certainly never conceived of such a role for the Court in such controversies."[60]

On October 7, 1985, the United States dropped the other shoe, by giving notice of the termination of its acceptance of compulsory jurisdiction under article 36(2) of the Statute of the International Court of Justice. Despite earlier assurances by U.S. presidents—from Taft to Eisenhower—that Americans would rather lose a case than undermine the fledgling system of international adjudication, the United States had not proven a gracious loser. Washington attacked the decision as "contrary to law and fact" and impugned the tribunal by charging that it could not present "sensitive material...before a Court that includes two judges from Warsaw Pact nations."[61] The counselor for legal affairs to the U.S. Mission to the UN concluded that "the process of setting a good example does not yield results— not, at least, in terms of getting others to follow our example in accepting the compulsory jurisdiction of the Court. . . ."[62] He went on to question whether U.S. freedom of action in its national self-interest should ever be restricted by deference to any world court.

What was new about this was not so much the view being expressed. Rather, it was that the view was now emanating from the executive branch—for two hundred years the bastion of the multilateralist vision—rather than from a vociferous unilateralist minority in Congress.

To a considerable extent, the multilateralists have themselves to blame. Throughout a long campaign to implement their program, they repeatedly settled for self-contradictory compromises and fictions. Once the Connally reservation had been added, the 1946 Senate acceptance of the World Court's compulsory jurisdiction was little more than disguised rejection. When the multilateralists yielded to the Connally reservation, they effectively laid the groundwork for the justification now advanced for withdrawal—that the United States had tried to lead the world into the promised land of global recourse to international law and courts, but that few had followed.

In fact, forty-five states *have* accepted some form of article 36(2) jurisdiction; five have even emulated the U.S. "example" by doing so with a Connally-type reservation.[63] (It should be pointed out that the Connally reservation also boomeranged against the United States. Those states that have accepted the World Court's jurisdiction without qualification could avoid being sued by the

United States because the U.S. reservation operated reciprocally as a shield for its adversaries.)

But what sort of example has the United States really set for the world? Behind the facade of inflated rhetoric, logical conundrums, and legal fictions, it has *not* led the way and has *never* made a broad commitment to the principle of international adjudication. Thus, it should not be surprising that most other nations do not follow our "good example," because it is not seen to be one.

• 3 •

Remaining U.S. Ties to the World Court

If the United States were truly sovereign, it would have no treaties or other international agreements, the functional utility of which is to restrict the rights of the parties to do whatever they feel like, substituting the obligation of reciprocal, predictable, normative behavior. If the United States wished to be fully sovereign, it also would surely reject the World Court and all its works. But, instead, the United States adheres to thousands of treaties and agreements. It also continues to come under the jurisdiction of the World Court in many significant respects.

Just as the nation never really *accepted* the World Court's compulsory jurisdiction—in the sense that adherence to that jurisdiction under article 36(2) of the Statute of the International Court of Justice was rendered largely illusory, both by the Connally reservation and by an ambivalent attitude to the global vision—it has not really *rejected* the World Court, either, because its power over the United States was never primarily based on article 36(2) compulsory jurisdiction, even though that controversial provision has attracted the most attention.

In terminating U.S. acceptance of compulsory jurisdiction, the State Department announced that this "does not signify any diminution of our traditional commitment to international law and to the International Court of Justice in performing its proper functions. U.S. acceptance of the World Court's jurisdiction under Article 36(1) of its Statute remains strong. We are committed to the proposition that the jurisdiction of the Court comprises all cases which the parties refer to it and all matters that are appropriate for the Court to handle pursuant to the United Nations Charter or treaties and conventions in force. We will continue to make use of the Court to resolve disputes whenever appropriate and will encourage others to do likewise."[1]

The reference to "the jurisdiction of the Court" in matters "pursuant to the United Nations Charter or treaties and conventions" is taken literally from the terms of article 36(1). It therefore constitutes a binding treaty obligation on the United States, one that cannot be renounced except by leaving the United Nations, since the Statute of the International Court of Justice is part of the UN Charter. No reservations are permitted, and article 36(1) is not "optional" except in the sense that the United States need not sign any treaties that give the World Court jurisdiction. But, as we shall see, the United States has subscribed to many treaties that do exactly that.

In other words, even after renouncing the World Court's compulsory jurisdiction, the United States is still subject to its authority in a broad variety of potential disputes giving rise to article 36(1) jurisdiction. The State Department itself takes the position that we are party "to over sixty. . .treaties or agreements providing for ICJ resolution of disputes arising under them" and has observed that such cases "under treaties and specific agreements form by far the largest and most successful part of the Court's work. The President's decision [to renounce article 36(2) compulsory jurisdiction] has no effect in this area."[2]

Other experts have identified as many as seventy treaties that, in one way or another, oblige the United States to go to the World Court in disputes that may arise under them.[3] The actual number may be larger. No one knows for sure, since some of the agreements and treaties making provision for the World Court's jurisdiction may have fallen into desuetude, while others contain commitments to the World Court's jurisdiction that can be read to be less than binding. The bottom line, however, is that the United States continues to be subject to the World Court's mandatory jurisdiction in connection with the interpretation of legal obligations arising out of many international agreements. The provisions in those agreements referring disputes to the World Court cannot be renounced without renouncing or renegotiating the agreements themselves, most of which continue to serve the U.S. national interest.

These "treaty"-based submissions to the World Court's jurisdiction, in many instances, are just as "compulsory" as was the now-rejected jurisdiction of the World Court under article 36(2). The principal difference is that the "treaty" jurisdiction is limited to matters arising out of the context and substance of a treaty, whereas the general compulsory jurisdiction applies to any question of international law whatsoever. To that extent, the notice of termination of U.S. acceptance of compulsory jurisdiction under article 36(2) on October 7, 1985, has narrowed the U.S. commitment to the World Court.

Bilateral Agreements

Fred L. Morrison, professor of law at the University of Minnesota, has recently compiled a survey of seventy treaties to which the United States is a party and that contain clauses submitting disputes to the World Court.[4] He examines sixteen still-effective bilateral economic cooperation agreements concluded in the aftermath of World War II, fourteen with friendly West European states but others with Turkey and Israel. Typical is the agreement with Austria, by which that country and the United States "agree to submit to the decision of the International Court of Justice any claim espoused by either Government on behalf of one of its nationals against the other Government."[5]

This provision, which is intended to benefit nationals of one country living or doing business in the other, is hedged by a clause that states that the obligation to go to the World Court "is limited by the terms and conditions" of U.S. acceptance of the compulsory jurisdiction of the World Court under article 36(2). In effect, the clause incorporated the Connally reservation into these agreements, thereby limiting U.S. submission to the World Court in the way designated by the Senate in 1946. Oddly, now that the United States has terminated its acceptance of compulsory World Court jurisdiction, the Connally reservation may live on by incorporation into these agreements. Or it may have died, thereby paradoxically widening the World Court's jurisdiction over the United States in matters arising out of these treaties.

Morrison's survey also includes fifteen agreements, still in effect, made in the 1950s, when the United States embarked on an aggressive campaign to secure adoption of so-called treaties of Friendship, Commerce, and Navigation, also referred to as treaties of Amity or Establishment. These, too, seek to protect the citizens of the respective parties and ensure favorable treatment when a national of one party is in the territory of another. They create mutual rights to engage in commercial activities, own businesses, and inherit property. Typically, the agreements provide that any "dispute between the Parties after the interpretation or application of the present Treaty, not satisfactorily adjusted by diplomacy, shall be submitted to the International Court of Justice, unless the Parties agree to settlement by some other pacific means."[6]

Once again, the principal partners were the democratic nations of Western Europe, but treaties also were signed with China, Ethiopia, Iran, Israel, Japan, Korea, Nicaragua, Pakistan, Togo, and Vietnam. Not so incidentally, the agreement with Nicaragua constituted one of the jurisdictional bases on which that country took the United States to the World Court in 1984, asserting that U.S. military actions against the Sandinista regime violated the commitment to friendship and to free navigation. That agreement, belatedly, was terminated as of May 1, 1986.

The experience with Nicaragua is instructive. A presumed advantage to the United States of article 36(1) over article 36(2) is that the World Court has compulsory jurisdiction only in disputes between the United States and nations with which it chooses to have multilateral or bilateral agreements. But regimes change and friendly nations turn unfriendly, as in the cases of Iran, Ethiopia, and Nicaragua; there can be unpleasant surprises for each side. Just as the United States was surprised to be impleaded in 1984 under a treaty with Nicaragua, so the revolutionary government of Iran found itself unexpectedly impleaded under a treaty in connection with the hostage crisis in Tehran.[7]

Additional bilateral agreements that provide for some form of mandatory submission to the World Court include two consular conventions (with Belgium and Korea) and a treaty (with Canada) relating to cooperative development of the water resources of the Columbia River basin.[8] The treaty with Canada, however, only provides for recourse to the World Court as a last resort, and only if the parties, in a specific instance, agree.

Multilateral Treaties and Conventions

Morrison also identifies thirty-six multilateral agreements that involve some form of U.S. submission to the World Court. These are either "quasi-legislative" agreements that "codify" international law or "constitutive" agreements that establish international organizations and agencies. There are twenty-six "quasi-legislative" and ten "constitutive" multilateral agreements currently in effect that oblige the United States to use the World Court in disputes about the agreements' meaning or substance.[9]

"Quasi-legislative" agreements include Geneva conventions on the law of the sea and the conventions on narcotic drugs and on copyright.[10] "Quasi-legislative" multilateral agreements also deal with the protection of diplomats, the status of Antarctica, the settlement of investment disputes, the status of refugees, the protection of industrial property, the suppression of aircraft hijacking, the protection of the rights of women, the suppression of slavery, and the regulation of international road traffic.

In 1986, the Senate ratified the Genocide Convention,[11] another "quasi-legislative" agreement, but added a reservation nullifying U.S. acceptance of article 9, which gives the World Court compulsory jurisdiction over disputes "relating to the interpretation, application or fulfillment of the present Convention." While most international conventions, implicitly or explicitly, permit reservations at the time a state joins, they usually do not permit them subsequently. To escape the World Court's jurisdiction under existing treaties, the United States would probably have to abrogate adherence to the agreements, a move that might be against its national interest.

These "quasi-legislative" multilateral conventions form a series of interlacing nets that weave the fabric of the international legal system. As Morrison points out, the "United States has treaty relationships with virtually all nations under one or more of these conventions."[12] The United States invoked several of them to bring the hostage case against Iran before the World Court in 1980. Approximately twenty more multilateral agreements with clauses giving the World Court jurisdiction are currently under consideration in Washington.

The ten "constitutive" conventions to which the United States is a party include the Food and Agriculture Organization, the International Labor Organization, the International Atomic Energy Agency, the International Civil Aviation Organization, and the World Health Organization.[13]

Typical of this kind of "constitutive" agreement is article 75 of the constitution of the World Health Organization, which provides that any dispute concerning the interpretation or application of the agreement, if not settled by negotiation, "shall be referred to the International Court of Justice in conformity with the Statute of the Court, unless the parties concerned agree on another mode of settlement."

Evaluation

Since many multilateral conventions have over a hundred parties, by accepting such a convention the United States becomes committed to "accept the jurisdiction of the Court with respect to far more countries than . . . under the 'compulsory jurisdiction' clause of article 36(2),"[14] which was accepted by only forty-five other countries. Currently, the United States has obligations to submit to the World Court disputes with 31 nations under bilateral agreements and more than 160 nations under multilateral treaties and conventions.[15] Although the U.S. commitment to accept the jurisdiction of the World Court under these agreements is limited to the agreements' substance and terms, it is clear that the 1985 termination of U.S. adherence to article 36(2) left intact many of its ties to the tribunal.

That the article 36(1) ties are the most important is borne out by recent experience. Of the eleven cases brought to the World Court between 1962 and 1986, none was based solely on the general compulsory jurisdiction of article 36(2). In ten of the cases, the World Court's jurisdiction was grounded in treaties—i.e., they came before the court under article 36(1) jurisdiction, although three of these were additionally based on article 36(2). (In one other case jurisdiction was based on a different provision of the Statute of the International Court of Justice.)

Some American experts on the subject, concluding that the United States is far from having withdrawn from the World Court's compulsory jurisdiction, see this as a potential danger. Morrison, for one, believes that careful reconsideration should be given to the status of each of the agreements that apply article 36(1). Some treaties, he argues, leave open the possibility of "jurisdiction nearly as broad as that of an unlimited declaration" under article 36(2).[16]

In terminating U.S. adherence to article 36(2), however, the Department of State specifically declared its desire to continue to adhere to bilateral and multilateral treaty commitments involving the World Court's article 36(1) jurisdiction. As noted, U.S. participation in most of these cooperative arrangements reflects self-interest. Even the Soviet Union, which generally shuns the World Court, has joined in some multilateral treaties that have provisions for judicial settlement of disputes.

There are other reasons to keep these agreements in effect. Submission to article 36(2) exposed the United States to suit by any nation willing to make a similar general acceptance of the World Court's compulsory jurisdiction. For the most part, however, U.S. treaty commitments—at least the bilateral ones—extend to friendly nations with which it should not fear to litigate. Morrison, however, citing Nicaragua, observes that "[s]ome of the treaty partners are now among the states least favorably disposed to the United States"[17] and cautions policymakers to keep those sorts of commitments under constant review. Most are terminable at one year's notice.

It is important to keep in mind the distinction between the terminated U.S. obligations under article 36(2) and the continuing obligations under article 36(1). The kinds of disputes that can arise under article 36(2) are infinite in variety and unpredictable as to subject matter. The kinds of disputes that can arise under article 36(1) are circumscribed by the substance of specific treaties. The commitments the United States has made in treaties are undertaken with its eyes wide open, in the expectation of mutual benefit and in pursuance of deliberate, self-interested policy. They involve obligations and commitments the United States ought to be willing to keep. If the United States expects to carry out those freely assumed undertakings, the possibility of having disputes adjudicated should pose no unmanageable risk, particularly if the United States continues to review the obligations in the light of changing circumstances. This assumes, of course, that the United States intends to remain a law-abiding member of the international community and that the World Court is a benevolent institution that will administer impartial justice—assumptions that will be examined in the ensuing chapters.

• 4 •

The Case Against the World Court

From the perspective of the U.S. national interest, is the World Court a benevolent institution?

Measured against the baseline of high expectations for international law in general and for international adjudication in particular, the World Court's performance cannot but be rated as disappointing. In this respect, the World Court has shared the fate of the United Nations itself. Indeed, some of the disenchantment Americans have experienced toward the United Nations has simply carried over to other institutions of the international system. As an integral part of the UN family, no doubt some of the annoyance directed against the querulous General Assembly has affected public attitudes toward even so sedate and sequestered an institution as the World Court. And unrealistically high expectations, when unrealized, lead to unrealistically severe bouts of disillusionment.[1]

This is not to say that the World Court should be regarded as above criticism. But its performance should be measured against realistic criteria. A distinction also should be made between the performance of the World Court and the performance of states in misusing—or failing to use—it.

Three charges have been made that, if valid, must be accounted "failures" of the World Court: (1) that the judiciary is biased, (2) that the World Court has overreached its jurisdiction to become "political," and (3) that it is institutionally incapable of making the determinations of fact that are at the heart of most significant international disputes.

Judicial Bias

In 1984, at the annual meeting of the American Society of International Law, UN Ambassador Jeane Kirkpatrick charged that the World Court judges reflect the political biases and proclivities predominant in the political organs of the United Nations.[2]

She was subsequently supported in this view by Monroe Leigh, a former legal adviser in the Department of State. In a memorandum to a committee of the American Society of International Law, Leigh agreed with Kirkpatrick that the "selection procedure for judges and the composition of the Court has increased the impression of the Court as a political organization in which many, if not a majority of the members oppose U.S. interests."[3] He argued that the emergence of one hundred new states in the UN system has altered both the composition of the World Court and the attitudes of the judges. In 1946, for example, there were six judges from the Americas and four from Western Europe. At that time, also, the judges from China and Egypt reflected West European values. Today, by contrast, there are only three judges from the Americas—the same number as from Communist states. And there are "a significantly greater number of judges from nations that are at least sympathetic to interests adverse to those of the United States."[4]

Certainly, with the amendment of the UN Charter in 1963, the enlarged Security Council (like the General Assembly) began to reflect the predominance of Third World states. Leigh concludes that, because of the "large number of less developed states in the Assembly, it became necessary for judicial candidates to curry the favor of these nations whose interests and values are often different than U.S. interests and values." With the judges being elected on the same agenda and at the same time as members to various other UN bodies, he states, "it is inevitable that political bargaining occurs as the election of the candidate to the Court is traded off for support of another candidate to another body."[5]

The charge that World Court judges are biased or "politicized," and that they decide cases in reference to their subjective belief systems, is not one that would surprise students of the American judiciary—an institution frequently charged, by various interest groups, with being biased. To some degree, the charge against the World Court judges is probably true. The question is to what degree? As World Court Judge Levi Carneiro candidly admitted in his opinion in the Anglo-Iranian Oil Co. case, "It is inevitable that every one of us in this Court should retain some trace of his legal education and his former legal activities in his country of origin."[6] Article 9 of the Statute of the International Court of Justice enjoins "that in the body as a whole the representation of the main forms of civilization and of the principal legal systems of the world should be assured." Since the demography of the world has changed radically in the past four decades, the World Court has had to accommodate newly recognized "forms of civilization" and the new "legal systems" of Africa and Asia in a new ethnic and cultural mixture of judges.

It is perfectly legitimate for Americans to ask whether this shift is to the significant disadvantage of the United States. This is not a question yielding simple answers. Between its debut, in March 1948, and 1985, the World Court has rendered 115 decisions and advisory opinions. The U.S. judge voted with the majority in eighty-two of these, dissenting, in whole or in part, in only fifteen. (In ten instances, the U.S. judge was not present to vote, and in eight his vote was not recorded individually.) The U.S. judge dissented three times as often (in relation to the total number of decisions and opinions) since 1964, when the influence of the Third World in the World Court began to take effect, than in the earlier years. In the earlier period, the U.S. judge voted with the majority fifty-four times and dissented on five occasions; in the later period he sided with the majority twenty-eight times and dissented ten times. (See Appendix A.) Still, the total number of U.S. dissents is so small in each period that it may be of limited statistical significance.

An examination of the actual instances of dissent in the period 1964 to 1985, moreover, reveals that the American judge disagreed with the majority of the World Court in circumstances that often fail to confirm the contention of bias. In 1966, for example, the U.S. judge sided with the Liberian and Ethiopian plaintiffs against the Republic of South Africa, thereby agreeing with the Third World against a "Western" defendant. In 1974, the U.S. judge, in two related decisions, sided with New Zealand and Australia (plaintiffs) against France (defendant). In 1982, the U.S. judge dissented on a technical matter involving quasi-contractual claims of a UN employee against the organization. In 1985, the dissent of the U.S. judge in the Libya-Malta case was in no way related to a U.S. concern.

In none of these cases could the majority be said to have taken a position that was contrary in any way to the U.S. national interest. Only in 1984, in the two early phases of Nicaragua's action against the United States, was the U.S. judge in a position of dissenting in a matter of direct interest to his country. Even in those instances, it is difficult to view the majority-minority split as irrefutable evidence of judicial bias, since the U.S. judge, Stephen Schwebel, was not joined in dissent by judges from *any* states—not even those that may be presumed to share U.S.

cultural and ideological tendencies. The majority that decided against each U.S. contention included the West European and Latin American judges as well as judges from Communist and Afro-Asian nations. Even in the final (merits) phase of the Nicaraguan case, the U.S. judge was joined in dissent, for the most part, by the Japanese and British judges, but not by other "Western" judges from France, Norway, and Italy.

Nor can the allegation of prevailing judicial animosity to U.S. interests be sustained by two World Court decisions, handed down in 1979 and 1980, pertaining to the American hostages in Tehran. In the first of these, which dealt with "provisional measures," the World Court unanimously sided with the United States. In the second, the Soviet judge dissented, but the Polish one, except as to the subsidiary matter of damages owed to the United States, voted with the majority.[7]

Further, even before 1964, the World Court decided a case involving U.S. interests in such a way as to impel the U.S. judge to dissent. The 1952 case concerning the rights of nationals of the United States in Morocco—a dispute between the United States and France—also led to a decision with which the U.S. member of the World Court disagreed.

Nevertheless, the charge of judicial bias is as difficult to disprove as to prove. The mere presence on the World Court of judges "representing" the principal legal systems creates a reasonable assumption that a judge representing a socialist, as opposed to a capitalist, system of jurisprudence, or a judge from a developing as opposed to a developed country, would bring to cases differing jurisprudential preferences or values.

In many kinds of international disputes, however, the world's value systems are not so readily juxtaposed. No international judges from any civilized legal system could be presumed to believe that the kidnapping of diplomats is, or ought to be, legal. Thus while the possibility of bias may arise in connection with certain kinds of ideologically freighted disputes—such as a case concerning the right of a nationalized foreign corporation to full compensation from the nationalizing government—it will not arise in many other kinds of litigation. Further, the rules of the World Court now permit the parties to a dispute, if they agree, to choose to have the dispute heard before chambers of three, five, or more members of the bench, selected, in effect, by agreement between the litigants, rather than before the full fifteen-member bench.

Judicial Overreach

Critics also allege that World Court judges are increasingly deciding cases that do not belong in the World Court because these cases are essentially political, not legal.

Speaking on this issue to fellow members of the Supreme Court of the United States, Justice Frankfurter observed: "the court's authority—possessed of neither the purse nor the sword—ultimately rests on sustained public confidence in its moral sanction. Such feeling must be nourished by the court's complete detachment, in fact and in appearance, from political entanglements and by abstention from injecting itself into the clash of political forces in political settlements."[8] While this may sound reasonable in theory, Frankfurter's position was rejected in practice by the majority of judges in the case—*Baker v. Carr*—in which the words were spoken. The Supreme Court rejected the notion that it should not decide on the constitutionality of a state legislature's apportionment of its own voting districts because the issue was too "political." Neither the Supreme Court nor the World Court can altogether achieve "complete detachment from political entanglements."

Domestic cases concerning such issues as school desegregation, abortion, capital punishment, and the racial composition of juries are all "political" in the sense that the questions to be decided by the court have featured prominently in the halls of Congress, in state legislatures, and in election campaigns at every level. Similarly, the mining of the Straits of Corfu by Albania, South Africa's right to administer Namibia, France's right to test nuclear weapons in the Pacific, and the right of British trawlers to fish off Iceland, as well as questions raised by the holding of U.S. hostages in Iran and the U.S. support for Contra forces in Nicaragua all involve World Court judges in issues that are certainly the focus of repeated and heated debate in national and international political forums.

But until the Nicaraguan action was brought before the World Court, it had been the Soviet judge who, from time to time, had complained that the tribunal was deciding cases that were inappropriate because they were "inherently political." In a 1962 dissenting opinion concerning the legality of expenses incurred by the United Nations in its peacekeeping operations in the Suez and Congo—operations opposed by the Soviet Union—Judge Koretsky argued that the World Court ought to refuse to decide.

"First and foremost," he said, "we have there a political question. . . ." The court ought to abstain, he argued, otherwise, "its opinion may be used as an instrument of political struggle."[9]

While engaged in its losing battle with Nicaragua, the State Department, for the first time, resorted to the "political issue" argument.[10] "The conflict in Central America," the State Department said, "is not a narrow legal dispute; it is an inherently political problem that is not appropriate for judicial resolution." It added, "Nicaragua's suit against the United States—which includes an absurd demand for hundreds of millions of dollars in reparations—is a blatant misuse of the Court for political and propaganda purposes."[11]

Eugene V. Rostow, emeritus professor of international law at Yale, has argued in support of this position. In his opinion, the Nicaraguan claim against the United States turned on whether the World Court should replace the Security Council as the UN forum for resolving the dispute and whether the United States or the World Court has the right to determine when U.S. force is being used in self defense. Rostow maintains that in U.S. constitutional practice, such questions would be held by the Supreme Court to be political questions beyond its competence.[12]

Israeli scholar Shabtai Rosenne does not accept such a clear-cut distinction between the political and legal. "Litigation," he states, "is but a phase in the unfolding of a political drama. . . .The general development of every branch of international law has been the consequence of political events, so that the law itself is closely affected by the circumstances of international politics. . . .The assumed antithesis between law and politics commonly postulated for domestic state-organization is not fully relevant to international law and organization."[13]

The use of the term "political disputes" as a rationale for excluding judicial settlement has drawn the ire of the British former judge of the International Court of Justice, Sir Hersch Lauterpacht, who characterizes it as "a well-meant attempt to lend the authority of a legal principle to an attitude of States inimicable to any recognition of the sovereignty of law." He points out that the "State is a political institution and all questions which affect it as a whole, in particular its relations with other States, are therefore political." But if all such "political" matters were removed from the purview of judges, this "would mean a speedy and radical liquidation of the activities of the Court."[14]

As for the State Department charge of "propaganda," international legal decisions are widely acknowledged to be "enforced" primarily in the court of public opinion. That a losing party in a World Court case will become the victim of bad publicity is often the only expectation motivating resort to the court. It is somewhat disingenuous, therefore, to feign horror that Nicaragua has resorted to the World Court to gain a propaganda victory over the United States. Why did the United States sue Iran over its taking of diplomatic hostages if not to exert the weight of international public opinion on Tehran?

The debate over whether a particular dispute is essentially "political" or "legal" has a long history. The right question, though, is not whether the dispute is essentially legal or political but whether it is more likely to be settled by recourse to a political or a legal forum.

Is a settlement of the U.S. dispute with Nicaragua, for example, more likely to occur in the United Nation's political organs, the World Court, or neither? The General Assembly, with 160 members, is unlikely to be a forum for effective negotiations. In the Security Council, the United States has a veto and Nicaragua an automatic majority, which could, but rarely does, conduce to negotiated compromise. Outside the United Nations, the dispute has been before the "Contadora" group, a smaller negotiating forum of states of the region, but, so far, without visible success.

That does not necessarily make the World Court the best dispute settlement mechanism in the U.S.-Nicaraguan dispute. Its utility is sharply circumscribed by the fact that it cannot enforce a judgment that is unacceptable to one or both of the parties. In addition, judicial decisions tend to side with one party against the other, rather than arranging a compromise, which may be the sine qua non of a settlement. In other words, the dispute between Nicaragua and the United States may simply be of a kind that cannot be resolved by any UN or non-UN organ—political or juridical.

Hans Morgenthau, many years ago, correctly pointed to the real essence of the debate: "At the bottom of disputes which entail the risk of war, there is a tension between the desire to preserve the existing distribution of power and the desire to overthrow it. These conflicting desires. . . are rarely expressed in their own terms—terms of power—but in moral or legal terms. What the representatives of nations talk about are moral principles and legal claims, what their talk refers to are conflicts of power."[15]

Morgenthau correctly observes that to attempt to solve such problems in legal terms may simply aggravate the tensions that underlie them. In disputes with very high stakes, moreover, a powerful nation like the United States is unlikely to relinquish—either to an international judicial or political institution—its option to use force as a last resort in defense of its national interest. When such extraordinary circumstances prevail, the utility of any dispute-settling forum will be determined entirely by whether it encourages the parties themselves to negotiate with one another in good faith.

The World Court, in various cases, has emphatically rejected the notion that it is an inherently unsuitable umpire when a dispute might be characterized as essentially "political." In the Iran hostages case, the majority stated that ". . . legal disputes between sovereign States by their very nature are likely to occur in political contexts, and often form only one element in a wider and long-standing political dispute between the States concerned. Yet never has the view been put forward that, because a legal dispute submitted to the Court is only one aspect of a political dispute, the Court should decline to resolve for the parties the legal question at issue between them."[16]

Louis B. Sohn, professor of international law at the University of Georgia, arguing an aspect of the Nicaraguan case for the U.S. government, told the judges that it was "not the United States' purpose to argue that the application must be dismissed because it presents a 'political' question, as opposed to a legal question." "It is our purpose," he stated, "to demonstrate that the allegation upon which the Nicaraguan Application depends in its entirety, namely, that of an ongoing use of unlawful armed force, was never intended by the drafters of the Charter of the United Nations to be encompassed by Article 36(2) of the Statute of the Court."[17]

Like Justice Frankfurter, Sohn was inviting the Court to duck the dispute not because it was "political" but because the "clash of political forces" had reached such a point that, by mixing in, the judges were more likely to hurt the World Court than help the parties.

If the United States considers it in its own interest (and that of the World Court) to exclude from the purview of law and judges disputes that have waxed into actual military hostilities, it can readily achieve that result by reserving those disputes in any future submission to the World Court's article 36(2) compulsory jurisdiction. States already at war are notoriously reluctant to substitute trial by judges for trial by combat. But a court that never entertains a case, and never rules on a dispute, because it might get hurt—or worse, ignored—is far guiltier of being politicized than one that obeys the Latin maxim to "do justice 'tho the sky falls."

The Court as Finder of Facts

Bruce Rashkow, an assistant legal adviser at the State Department, has pointed to the Nicaraguan case as an example of the sort of dispute that turns primarily on allegations of fact. These, in the U.S. view, are really beyond the capability of a group of fifteen senior jurists ensconced at The Hague.

"In its written and oral pleadings before the Court," Rashkow has written, "Nicaragua makes numerous assertions that Honduras, Costa Rica, and El Salvador are acting in concert with the United States in using military force in violation of Nicaragua's sovereignty, territorial integrity, and political independence. Nicaragua, for example, contended that the United States had installed more than 10,000 mercenaries in more than ten camps in Honduras along the border with Nicaragua. Nicaragua asserted that there were 2,000 mercenaries supported by the United States operating against Nicaragua from Costa Rica and that the United States has bases, radar stations, spy planes, spy ships, and the armies of El Salvador and Honduras at its service."[18] Interestingly, the argument advanced by the government of Nicaragua has relied heavily on accounts in U.S. newspapers. But as the American side put it, "newspaper accounts concerning what may or may not be taking place are inherently unsatisfactory even as historical, let alone legal, evidence."[19] How can the World Court judges sort out fact from fiction in a situation so remote and obscure?

The United States contended that Nicaragua is using military force against its neighbors, "violating their sovereignty, territorial integrity, and political independence." Rashkow argues that the United States has information to support these allegations, but that "many of the facts at its disposal are based upon information that it must strictly control for reasons of national security."[20] Moreover, "even if the United States. . .were willing to provide some of this information to the Court on a confidential basis, it is doubtful that the Court would permit them to do so." In any event, "the Court faces enormous difficulties in determining the facts in a situation of ongoing armed conflict."[21]

Completing his indictment, Rashkow asks: "How then is the Court to determine the facts? Is the Court to call its own witnesses? To whom are they to talk and under what circumstances? Which of the many political parties and dissident groups? With whom among these often divided groups are they to speak? Is the Court to make on-site visits? Where are they to visit? Which country? Which city, village or jungle encampment? When and under what circumstances are they to visit?" He concludes that whether or not "the Court has the theoretical authority to deal with these problems of fact-finding, it is clear, as a practical matter, they cannot effectively deal with the factual issues raised by Nicaragua's complaint, certainly not during ongoing hostilities."[22]

American lawyers involved in the Nicaragua case have been at pains to point out that the rules of the World Court do not permit the kind of "discovery" before trial that is used by the parties in U.S. litigation to compel opponents to disgorge relevant information that may be peculiarly within the possession of an adversary. This complaint and accompanying negative view of the World Court's fact-finding capabilities have been rebutted by legal practitioners—including some American practitioners—who point out that despite the absence of pretrial discovery procedures, the World Court has extraordinarily wide latitude in procuring and examining evidence. Keith Highet, the current president of the American Society of International Law and frequently a counsel before the World Court, has expressed the view that the "breadth and flexibility" of article 48 of the Statute of the International Court of Justice, which provides that it "shall make orders for the conduct of the case, shall decide the form and time in which each party must conclude its arguments, and make all arrangements connected with the taking of evidence," enables the World Court "to act with a surprising degree of responsiveness to various questions of fact presented to it for resolution."[23]

The World Court is equipped with authority to call upon each party to a dispute to produce specific evidence. It can commission inquiries, request expert opinions, and examine witnesses (even away from the seat of the court).[24] While the World Court cannot order evidentiary production, subpoena witnesses, or punish for contempt, it has, in part, remedied this deficiency by imposing a strict burden of proof on the plaintiff. As Rosenne states, "the Court will formally require the party putting forward a claim to establish the elements of facts and law on which decision in its favor might be given."[25] Then—as occurred during the Nicaraguan proceedings—if one of the parties refuses to participate, the World Court is required to take the initiative to satisfy itself "that the claim is well founded in fact and law."[26] Legal observers have noted that in the Nicaragua case, the World Court frequently engaged in active cross-examination of witnesses produced by Nicaragua, in an effort to compensate for the absence of U.S. counsel.

In making its own search for relevant evidence, the World Court is authorized by rule 62 of the Court's Rules of Procedure to call upon parties at any time to "produce such evidence or to give such explanations as the Court may consider to be necessary for the elucidation of any aspect of the matter in issue, or may itself seek other information for this purpose." The judges may also seek relevant information from international organizations.[27] This lays the foundation for a far more active judicial role than is common in U.S. trial courts. Lauterpacht has observed that "the Court is in a position to perform that task with exacting care."[28]

The World Court has demonstrated its ability to assess huge and contradictory mountains of evidence concerning highly complex situations. In the Western Sahara case the judges, acting on the eve of the outbreak of military hostilities, were able to find a coherent pattern of facts from which contemporary title to that disputed territory might be pronounced in law.[29] The judges have unraveled voluminous historical records as well as demographic, ethnographic, and cartographic evidence in order to make decisions regarding the disputed status of frontier lands between Czechoslovakia and Poland, the status of a part of the Albanian frontier, the status of eastern Greenland, sovereignty over frontier lands between Belgium and the Netherlands, title to two islands in the English Channel, title to a religious shrine on the Cambodia-Thailand boundary, disputes between Tunisia and Libya, and Libya and Malta, concerning title to the continental shelf, as also between nations bordering on the North Sea, and pertaining to disputed fishery grounds in the Gulf of Maine.[30]

While there have only been eight cases in sixty years in which live witnesses and experts have appeared before the World Court, these hearings demonstrated considerable flexibility and acumen on the part of the judges.[31] In the Corfu Channel case, a military dispute between Albania and the United Kingdom over Albania's mining of that waterway, the World Court appointed a committee of experts to collect and evaluate logistic and even acoustic evidence. Three senior naval officers from Norway, Sweden, and Holland were sent to the disputed strait by the judges and filed a report establishing numerous subtle facts in an effort to clarify who did what and when.[32]

What about the problem of gathering facts during an "ongoing armed conflict?" The United States, in refusing to participate in the merits phase of the Nicaraguan case, correctly pointed out that the World Court has never attempted to judge a dispute in which the parties are still involved in actual combat. Some argue that the World Court cannot judge "fluid"—i.e., ongoing hostile—situations because the facts are constantly changing, making a judicial determination based on the facts at any given moment irrelevant by the time the judgment is uttered.[33] Others argue that the World Court cannot expect to examine the facts pertaining to a war that, at the time of litigation, is still being fought. While the World Court has the authority to examine a situation "on the spot," it can hardly be expected, for example, to tramp around the jungles on the Honduran-Nicaraguan border looking for Contra action.

Even if valid, neither argument leads inevitably to the conclusion that cases involving ongoing hostilities cannot be resolved before a competent court, only that they present special evidentiary problems. In a case like the one brought by Nicaragua, reliable evidence is extraordinarily difficult to obtain, and all testimony should be treated with skepticism. Since the onus of proof is on the party bringing the action—in this instance, Nicaragua—if the evidence was unreliable, secondhand, "frozen" in time and therefore obsolete, or simply impossible to verify because of the exigencies of wartime, then those would have been excellent arguments for the United States to have made in court at the time. However, the United States chose not to participate in the merits phase, when these issues could have been raised.

Even in conflicts where reliable independent verification is impossible, the facts may not always be in dispute. The U.S. government openly admitted to Congress that it mined the harbors of Nicaragua. Since that fact was not in dispute between the two litigants, the World Court need not have secured evidence to determine its truth. Another fact that was not in dispute was Nicaraguan involvement in the El Salvador civil war. Nicaragua's key witnesses admitted to the World Court that the Sandinistas, at least until 1981, had aided the El Salvador insurgents.[34] In addition, a recent study by John Norton Moore, one of the U.S. counsel in the early stages of the Nicaraguan litigation, illustrates how much public evidence of aggression against El Salvador—some of it from Nicaraguan officials themselves—was available for the United States to present to the World Court judges.[35] Thus, it should not invariably be assumed that the existence of armed conflict makes it impossible for a court to gather evidence.

Even if some facts cannot be ascertained in a timely fashion, that does not mean that a tribunal is necessarily paralyzed. When the World Court decided in favor of the United States in the Iranian hostages case, for example, it did not have every possible piece of relevant evidence. For one thing, the Iranians, in that instance, refused to come to the World Court at all. And the World Court was hardly of a mind to visit Iran for an on-the-spot investigation of the facts. Nevertheless, the judges had little difficulty in concluding, virtually unanimously, that the "essential facts of the. . .case are, for the most part, matters of public knowledge which have received extensive coverage in the world press and in radio and television broadcasts from Iran and other countries. . . . The result is that the Court has available to it a massive body of information from various sources concerning the facts and circumstances of the present case, including numerous official statements of both Iran and the United States authorities."[36]

As for the argument that the fluidity of events in combat situations makes judicial determination irrelevant, Highet has observed that "all situations are 'ongoing' even if the actions are done and in the past, as long as the possibility exists that a new and separate—although related—action may be undertaken which would cure the past action, or remedy the breach of an international obligation."[37] No inherent incapacity of the World Court to deal with such cases has been proved.

The Court's Vanishing Clientele

There exists a general unwillingness of states to take matters of national importance to international adjudication. In submitting to the compulsory jurisdiction of the World Court, the United States was in a small minority of states willing to grant such broad powers to the tribunal—and, with Britain, alone among the Big Five to do so. Even among states that have accepted the World Court's compulsory jurisdiction, there is a growing tendency to refuse to be hailed before its judges or to carry out their decisions once rendered. This is not necessarily a reflection on the World Court and its capabilities, but is certainly relevant in determining its utility in conducting U.S. foreign relations.

In the words of Allan Gerson, a deputy assistant attorney general who was legal adviser to the U.S. Mission to the United Nations, only a "minority of U.N. members have accepted the compulsory jurisdiction of the court, and many of these have expressly withheld from the court authority to decide issues affecting their national security—at least without the joint consent of all concerned parties. None of the so-called great powers have unqualifiably acceded to the court's jurisdiction on such matters." As to compliance with the World Court's decisions, Gerson observes that in 1962, the Soviet Union refused to comply with a judgment of the World Court that members pay their assessed share of UN peacekeeping operations; in 1973, France, which had accepted the compulsory jurisdiction of the World Court, refused to appear before the court to respond to Australia's and New Zealand's claims that its testing of nuclear devices in the South Pacific was unlawful. In fact, while the case was pending, France revoked its acceptance of the World Court's jurisdiction, foreshadowing the U.S. action in the Nicaraguan case.[38]

In its statement announcing the U.S. decision to terminate its acceptance of the compulsory jurisdiction of the World Court under article 36(2), the State Department said: "When President Truman signed the U.S. declaration accepting the World Court's optional compulsory jurisdiction on August 14, 1946, this country expected that other states would soon act similarly. . . .Unfortunately, few other states have followed our example. Fewer than one-third of the world's states have accepted the Court's compulsory jurisdiction, and the Soviet Union and its allies have never been among them. Nor, in our judgment, has Nicaragua. Of the five Permanent Members of the U.N. Security Council only the U.S. and the United Kingdom have submitted to the Court's compulsory jurisdiction. [This] has been deeply disappointing. We have never been able to use our acceptance of compulsory jurisdiction to bring other states before the Court, but have ourselves been sued three times."[39]

There can be no gainsaying the contention that states' receptivity to the World Court's services in the years since 1946 has been acutely disappointing. By the end of 1939, the "optional clause" giving the Permanent Court of International Justice, the World Court's predecessor, compulsory jurisdiction had been adopted by forty out of fifty-two states belonging to the League of Nations—nearly 70 percent of the members.[40] In comparison, by July 31, 1984, only forty-seven states—45 out of 160 members of the United Nations (fewer than 30 percent) and two nonmembers, Liechtenstein and Switzerland—had accepted the "optional clause," article 36(2) of the Statute of the International Court of Justice. As Leo Gross, professor of international law at The Fletcher School of Law and Diplomacy, has noted, while "the nominal international judicial community increased, the percentage of States accepting the Optional Clause declined."[41] Moreover, among the accepting states, many have made reservations exempting certain kinds of disputes, ranging from those between members of the British Commonwealth to those involving the use of armed forces.

While all this is, no doubt, disappointing from the perspective of world order and the promotion of dispute settlement, the current U.S. disappointment with the World Court based on the performance of other states is misplaced. As we have seen, the Connally reservation made the United States's "good example" largely illusory. What we gave the World Court with one hand, we took back with the other. By rights, the United States should, all along, have been counted among the states that never actually accepted article 36(2).

This is more than a matter of semantics. When U.S. government lawyers state that the United States has been unable to use its acceptance of compulsory jurisdiction to sue others, it is not necessarily because those others have not accepted the compulsory jurisdiction of the World Court. For example, on one occasion, the United States had to drop an action against Bulgaria, not because of Bulgaria's failure to accept the World Court's jurisdiction, but because, under the terms of the Statute of the International Court of Justice, it was able to use the Connally reservation against the United States. On several other occasions, as well, the State Department has been unable to use the World Court to bring a claim because of the reciprocal protection offered the other party by the Connally reservation.

States adhering to the World Court's compulsory jurisdiction under article 36(2) do so only in respect of other states accepting the same obligation. It is, therefore, nonsense to say that the United States, by joining the minority of states adhering to article 36(2), adopted an asymmetrical relationship that placed it at a severe disadvantage in relation to the large majority of states that had not. The U.S. obligation, to the extent it was an obliga-

• 5 •

How Useful Is the World Court?

At least as far as Americans are concerned, the World Court did not do itself a favor when it dismissed opportunities to duck the case brought by Nicaragua against the United States. No doubt the majority of judges believed themselves bound in law and honor not to turn a deaf ear to demands for justice by a small state claiming to have been victimized by a more powerful one. But in giving Nicaragua the benefit of several procedural and jurisdictional doubts, the World Court put itself into a position of fundamentally damaging its relations with its most important constituent: the United States.

The damage is now done. But the World Court's decision on the merits of the Nicaraguan case and the U.S. decision to reject the World Court's compulsory jurisdiction do *not* necessarily mean that the U.S. national interest requires a complete, final break with international law and adjudication. Instead, it calls for calm reassessment of when that system of laws and of judges serves the U.S. national interest and when it does not. The central issue is whether it is ever in the interest of the United States to have recourse to international adjudication and, if so, in what circumstances and under what conditions.

When a state accepts the compulsory jurisdiction of the World Court—whether under article 36(1) or 36(2)—it renounces alternative options that it would otherwise be free to employ. It is not a step to be taken lightly by any nation—least of all by a superpower with responsibility for the defense of the free world. To some extent, the United States already has limited that freedom of choice by adhering to the UN Charter. Article 2(3) obliges all members to "settle their international disputes by peaceful means in such a manner that international peace and security, and justice, are not endangered," and article 2(4) requires states to refrain from the use or threat of force. Still, when the United States gets into a dispute with another state, it does have a choice of means by which to try to affect the outcome.

There are many alternatives to the judicial process that do not involve recourse to military force and that are entirely permitted by international law and the UN Charter: bilateral negotiations; mediation; use of the "good offices" of a skilled troubleshooter, such as the United Nations' secretary-general; employment of neutral fact finders; or submitting disputes to a standing bilateral commission, such as the one established by Canada and the United States. A dispute also can be put before the Security Council in an effort to mobilize international public opinion. There is the option of going to arbitration and, finally, it is always possible to yield.

When is it in the national interest to renounce all these options in favor of the judicial process? One obvious answer: when the other options are less likely to produce a more favorable result. But can we identify more specifically the circumstances that make recourse to the international judicial process propitious?

Characteristics of Judicial Dispute Settlement

Richard Bilder, professor of international law at Wisconsin University Law School, has identified some characteristics unique to international adjudication.[1]

• *Judicial dispute settlement is principled.* Judicial decision applies general concepts derived from past disputes. By setting forth these principles in writing, the tribunal implies that they are likely to be applied to similar disputes in the future. Thus, in addition to providing a solution to a dispute, judicial dispute settlement develops a reasoned system of general guidelines called law. As a predictive tool ("if A then B"), law reduces uncertainty and surprise in international relations—a considerable benefit in the nuclear age.

• *Judicial dispute settlement is an ongoing process.* Even when a judicial decision goes against a disputant, that party reasonably can hope that at some future time, when "the shoe is on the other foot," the tribunal will apply the same principles to its benefit.

This expectation of future benefit may soften the blow of losing. Further, if the expectation of continuity is realized, a side-benefit is that international relations gradually become systematized and normative, raising the costs of—and reducing recourse to—"surprising" behavior. (The costs of anti-normative behavior tend to rise because it is resented by states that have a stake in the violated norm.) Another side-benefit is that every time a case is taken to the World Court, the system is reinforced as a "habit" of state behavior. Each time the World Court resolves a dispute, it increases the prospect for other cases being submitted to it. Every time a World Court decision is obeyed, that reinforces the fledgling international "habit" of compliance. Of course, the converse also is true.

• *Judicial dispute settlement is authoritative and impersonal.* The decisions of eminent jurists carry considerable global prestige. The winner's cause tends to be legitimated in the eyes of most of the world. Especially when World Court judgments are handed down by a large majority of the judges, it is difficult for the losing party to escape public opinion, and such decisions become particularly influential.

The prestige of the World Court also can conduce to settlement. Even when a negotiated settlement has been precluded by domestic politics, a government that cannot openly "bargain away" claims may be able to retreat before "the majesty of the law."

• *Judicial dispute settlement takes time.* Because the judicial process is comparatively slow and expensive, it may have the positive effect of creating a "cooling-off period." Putting a dispute into "cold storage" creates the time and incentive for parties to negotiate a settlement out of court. An aggressive litigating strategy can keep a case under judicial review for years, creating a "quiet zone" for bilateral negotiations outside the judicial process. While the World Court is proceeding with a case, it is also likely that both parties will deescalate whatever behavior has given rise to the dispute. To reinforce this tendency, the World Court sometimes has issued "interim relief," which enjoins all parties from taking actions that make the dispute worse.

• *Judicial dispute settlement may be a "zero-sum" game.* In most domestic U.S. litigation, one side wins and the other loses. While this has the merit of clarity and simplicity, it precludes compromise or reconciliation. When compromise is necessary to secure genuine settlement of a dispute, litigation may have serious drawbacks. That is why courts are often supplanted by less formal processes, such as arbitration, mediation, and conciliation. It also explains why, in U.S. courts, cases are so often settled before they are decided by a judge. The very possibility of a winner-take-all solution makes the mere threat of judicial settlement an inducement to informal negotiation.

The World Court, however, is unusual among courts of justice in its potential flexibility. It has developed some skill at bringing about compromise solutions when it is authorized to do so by the disputing parties. The World Court also has been used in a quasi-mediating capacity when asked by disputants to enunciate the legal principles relevant to a conflict without actually applying them. By this arrangement, at the end of the legal proceedings, the parties are left free to negotiate the settlement of their dispute on the basis of guidelines set forth by the World Court judges.

• *Judicial dispute settlement is conservative.* Courts, whether or not technically bound by precedents, tend to reason from the past to the present. What has been declared to be law in the past is likely to be applied in the present and projected into the future. Socialist and some Third World states have complained that judicial dispute settlement essentially perpetuates the global status quo. Whether the international judicial process is in the U.S. national interest depends, in part, on whether the United States intends to pursue a global strategy consistent with existing normative expectations or whether it will seek radical change in permissible international behavior.

Until quite recently, it has been conventional wisdom that the U.S. government obeys international law and that a strong international legal order is therefore congruent with its national interest. The essentially conservative nature of U.S. interests is indicated by America's predominant stake in the economic and political status quo. In the past five years, however, this conventional wisdom increasingly has been challenged within the Reagan administration and in public discourse.

The Implications

When the unique characteristics of the judicial process are counterproductive to dispute settlement and/or development of the law, then the parties to the dispute should seek other means of settlement. For example, if the parties to a dispute wish to keep future options open and relations flexible—that is, if they are prepared to settle a specific problem, yet wish to do so without "making a rule"—a bilaterally negotiated settlement, or one worked out through the "good offices" of the UN secretary-general may be preferable. Because negotiated settlement need not—but a judicial decision invariably must—spell out the principles on which the decision is based, the prospect that a rule will emerge may be the principal incentive, or disincentive, to a settlement.

Another rule of thumb is that a case is appropriate for judicial dispute settlement when the potential ratio of law to substance is high. A dispute involving small assets but large, unresolved questions of law is ordinarily more amenable to judicial dispute settlement than one involving enormous stakes but trivial, or well-settled, issues of law. When the questions raised by a case are of intense national interest to the parties, or primarily involve applying clear, established rules of law to complex facts, other methods of settlement may be indicated.

The amount of international law that can be made by a judicial decision is not related to the amount of goods, the intensity of the national interests, or the depth of passions involved in the outcome of the case. A relatively minor case—for example, a case concerning the expropriation of a modest foreign-owned asset, or an ambassador's duty-free privileges—may make more law than a major case—for example, a dispute concerning title to half a nation's territory. Since the World Court's special talent is in declaring the applicable law through principled reasoning, a high law-to-substance ratio indicates a dispute in which employing the World Court will probably benefit both the parties and the international legal system.

The ability to rely on the long-term applicability of the neutral principles enunciated by the World Court is one of the chief utilities of judicial dispute settlement. But such reliance can only be extended toward other states that have accepted a continuing reciprocal obligation to go to the World Court. If state B, in bringing an action against state A, only accepts the jurisdiction of the World Court one day before launching its litigation, and terminates it the day after judgment, that expectation is frustrated. Consequently, litigation is indicated between states that share a long-term commitment to the World Court; it is generally not indicated in disputes where one party has accepted the World Court's jurisdiction for the purposes of a single case. Such reliance is one of the advantages of the judicial process over ad hoc arbitration, and a large part of the reason why a world court came to be preferred to the Permanent Court of Arbitration.

The authority and prestige carried by World Court decisions (particularly if delivered by a large majority) make resort to judicial dispute settlement useful in cases in which domestic political acquiescence to a negotiated settlement may be difficult to obtain. Even though bilateral negotiations may reach the same result, there are times when only a prestigious world court can make the solution politically acceptable.

The tendency of litigation to cast disputes in winner-take-all terms suggests that the judicial process is more suitable for disputes in which compromise is unacceptable to one or both parties. A dispute over title to an airplane, for example, usually must be resolved in favor of one claimant or the other; neither disputant is likely to favor an order to operate the craft jointly. On the other hand, if the parties prefer a compromise solution, they may still seek it in court, but only if they have worked out an agreement that poses the dispute to the World Court so as to direct the court to seek a compromise or they have agreed to limit the World Court to enunciating the law, leaving themselves free to apply the law to the dispute in a negotiated settlement.

Challenge to the Legal Order

Traditional U.S. support for the international legal system has been challenged by the emergence of a "Reagan doctrine" that proposes revision of some of the most fundamental norms of the existing legal order. Reasonable persons can disagree on the wisdom of the Reagan doctrine, as well as over the viability of the traditional norms. One cannot, however, reasonably defend a national strategy that seeks to implement a radical new doctrine of state behavior while leaving itself open to judgment by the judicial guardians of the traditional norms.

The Reagan doctrine is a response to the Marxist-Leninist idea of "revolution without boundaries." Since the end of World War II, most global conflict between Communist and democratic forces has taken the form of civil wars, fought in several dozen nominally independent nations of Europe, Latin America, Africa, and Asia. The Greek civil war, the first of the series, began even before the unconditional surrender of Germany. Since then, the phenomenon has become endemic. Civil wars are currently under way in El Salvador, Nicaragua, Afghanistan, Ethiopia, Angola, Peru, Cambodia, Sri Lanka, and elsewhere. Insurgency on so global a scale has compelled U.S. leaders to make new tactical choices. The options include ignoring the whole thing behind a policy of "fortress America," shoring up threatened friendly or democratic states, retaliating against the sponsors of proxy wars, carrying proxy wars to shaky parts of opponents' dominions, or pursuing a combination of these and other strategies.

Not all of these options, however, are equally lawful. Traditional international legal doctrine favors established governments

over rebels. It has permitted aid to recognized regimes while pro-
hibiting outside help to insurgents.[2] Only if the rebels attain ap-
proximate parity with government forces—in military control
of territory and ability to exercise effective administration over
a fixed population—may international law be said to impose an
obligation of neutrality on outsiders. If a state provides help to
an insurgency, other states may use force not only against the
insurgents but also against their sponsor.[3]

In recent years, there have been various challenges to these
traditional norms. Some legal scholars have begun to assert that
treaty law—specifically article 2(4) of the UN Charter—prohibits
all outside intervention in any civil war, whether on the side
of the government or the insurgents.[4] The Soviets have come up
with what is popularly known as the "Brezhnev doctrine," which
claims the right to put down insurrection against socialist
regimes and the "Khrushchev doctrine," which claims the right
to export global revolution by giving aid to socialist insurgents.[5]

The United States, together with most of the non-Communist
world, long resisted these challenges to traditional law.[6] Then,
however, in mid-1984, Jeane Kirkpatrick, speaking in her official
capacity as U.S. ambassador to the United Nations and as a
member of the Reagan administration, signaled a significant
change that has become the basis of the Reagan doctrine. Point-
ing out that the Soviets had never played by the traditional rules,
she proposed a new policy of U.S. help for "democratic forces"—
whether governments or insurgents—fighting for "human rights"
against totalitarian forces. "Some assert that it is inconsistent
for the U.S. to support an insurgency against a government in
Nicaragua," she told the National Press Club, "and a government
against an insurgency in El Salvador. The answer is in both cases
that we are supporting legitimate democracy against those who
would base their powers on force. . . . A government which takes
power by force has no legitimate grounds for complaint against
those who would wrest power from it by force."[7]

Within the Reagan administration, there have been visible rifts
in public pronouncements. The president himself has claimed
a radical new U.S. right to fight fire with fire by supporting the
overthrow of the Sandinista regime. Others assert a more traditional right to respond in proportionate collective self-defense
(permitted by article 51 of the UN Charter) to interdict Nicaraguan
aid to the Salvadoran rebels, but not to overthrow the government in Managua.

Whether or not the United States should have made use of
the court in the Nicaraguan case depends in part on which right

the Reagan administration is asserting in its backing of the Contras: the radical or the traditional one. Those State Department lawyers who wanted to fight the Nicaraguan law suit believed that the United States, supported by the evidence, could win with reference to the traditional international law of collective self-defence. By contrast, the political strategy advanced by Kirkpatrick, and now seemingly embraced by most of the administration, requires quite another legal strategy. Had the United States gone into the World Court claiming a *right* to oust the Sandinista regime, its argument would have been rejected. The World Court is, above all, a conservative institution, unlikely to embrace so radical a departure from established norms. Before embarking on a Reagan doctrine, the United States should have taken care that its legality could not be tested in the World Court. The lesson is this: If the United States intends to pursue a foreign policy based, in significant part, on new principles at sharp variance with traditional norms, it should first protect itself against being brought before so inevitably inhospitable a forum as the World Court.

If it is embarked on overthrowing the Sandinista regime in the belief that nothing less will curb the Marxist propensity for exporting revolution, it should concurrently have abrogated the treaty of Friendship, Commerce and Navigation with Nicaragua and excepted from its submission to the World Court's compulsory jurisdiction all issues arising out of its use of force. Failing to bring its legal strategy into line with its political strategy, the United States found itself inevitably on the losing end of a major law suit.

Congruence between political and legal strategy will become even more urgent if those who direct U.S. foreign policy decide not merely to transform and radicalize the international system, but to ignore it altogether, in pursuit of a foreign policy based primarily on "targets of opportunity" and unbridled, narrowly perceived "self-interest." Such a policy decision has not yet been made. But this is the direction in which the United States may be drifting.

This is indicated by the nation's recent indifference to treaty obligations pertaining to UN financing. Article 17 of the UN Charter imposes a legal duty on all members to join in defraying the costs of the organization in accordance with a formula developed, at U.S. urging, by the General Assembly. In the mid-1960s, the Soviet Union, nevertheless, began to withhold a part of its assessed contribution, claiming that certain UN peacekeeping activities were unconstitutional (i.e., went beyond the powers of the organization as set out in the UN Charter). At the time, Ambassador Arthur Goldberg reserved for the United States the same right to withhold for cause. This "Goldberg corollary" has been used to hold back small parts of the U.S. annual dues in protest against certain UN activities, such as support for the Palestine Liberation Organization.

Since 1986, however, the United States has begun to hold back its contributions in general and on a very large scale. It is currently estimated to be on the verge of a $70 million default for 1986-87. It has not sought to justify these unilateral, across-the-board withholdings by objection to specific UN programs. Rather, they were legislatively mandated by Congress in the "Kassebaum amendment," the Gramm-Rudman-Hollings law, and section 151 of the 1986-87 Foreign Relations Authorization Act (the "Sundquist amendment").

The cuts made by Congress clearly violate U.S. legal obligations under the UN Charter. They evince a new, radical mood of indifference to international law and a preference for unilateral action in pursuit of the national interest. It is noteworthy that these initiatives to reject not merely certain aspects of relatively fluid customary law, but also solemn treaty commitments, are originating not with the administration but with Congress. Neither the State Department nor the president has begun to reassert primacy in the conduct of this aspect of U.S. foreign relations. Once again, U.S. policy is in danger of becoming a hydra-headed force in which everyone and no one would appear to be in charge. Inevitably, a coherent legal strategy is impossible in the absence of a coherent political one.

• 6 •

Recommendations

In a recent World Court case involving a dispute over title to the underwater continental shelf between Libya and Malta, Libya asked the court to bear in mind the much larger land-mass—and, by implication, population—of Libya and to apply the concept of "distributive justice."[1] Rejecting outright the proposition that it should fashion law as a vehicle for equalizing wealth, the majority opinion, by fourteen votes to three, flatly proclaimed "there can be no question of distributive justice" on the ground that such "considerations are totally unrelated to the underlying intention of the applicable rules of international law." The World Court must apply "not abstract justice but justice according to the rule of law; which is to say that its application should display consistency and a high degree of predictability. . . . It is clear that neither the rules determining the validity of legal entitlement to the continental shelf, nor those concerning delimitation between neighboring countries, leaves room for any consideration of economic development of the States in question."[2]

Significantly, this "conservative" view of the judicial function was shared by World Court judges across the spectrum of nationalities and ideologies: socialists, judges from Third World countries, and West Europeans and other free marketeers. To the extent that the United States may be embarking on a foreign policy incorporating radical theories of state conduct, therefore, it is prudent not to permit that conduct to be subject to World Court judicial veto.

International common law is shaped gradually by evolving patterns of states' behavior. The very rule that was applied in the Libya-Malta case—ownership of the submerged continental shelf by coastal states—while now universally accepted as a principle of sea law, was once a radical departure from the concept of the seas as "res nullius," incapable of being owned by any state. The departure was initiated forty years ago in a unilateral proclamation by President Truman that appropriated the U.S. coastal shelf to a depth of two hundred meters.[3] Had the Truman proclamation been tested before the World Court at its inception, in 1945, it might very well have been nullified as contrary to the norms of that time.

The Reagan doctrine represents a far more radical departure from prevailing law. Since Reagan's 1985 State of the Union address, American support for anti-Communist revolution is perceived as the "centerpiece of a revived and revised policy of containment" and "rolling back" of communism.[4] To the extent that the Reagan doctrine proclaims a right to take the offensive by aiding anti-Communist insurgencies, coupled with an asserted right to aid non-Communist regimes dealing with indigenous Marxist rebellions, it parallels the "Khrushchev doctrine," but departs from the norms generally accepted by the large majority of non-Communist states.

Supporters of the Reagan doctrine argue—as the State Department did in terminating U.S. acceptance of article 36(2) jurisdiction by the World Court—that the United States has tried adherence to traditional international law in respect to insurgencies and proxy wars, but that U.S. self-restraint has not been requited. They contend that "continued reliance on traditional internationalist means, such as the U.N. . . . as a *substitute* for American action . . . is, in fact, to choose a new and ill-disguised form of isolationism."[5] International law and institutions, they claim, by failing to enforce customary law and the rules of nonintervention set out in the UN Charter and General Assembly resolutions, have given the Soviets a free hand while the United States has too long responded with its hands tied behind it.

This argument overlooks U.S. involvement, as early as 1954, in anti-socialist insurgency in Guatemala. But to those who accept the logic of untying America's hands, it is but a short step to total rejection of World Court jurisdiction over any U.S. actions.

That conclusion is not a necessary concomitant of accepting the Reagan doctrine. If the United States intends to change existing customary practice relating to use of its military power, it should withdraw from the jurisdiction of the World Court all matters pertaining to its discretion in the use of force. But it should continue to subject itself to the World Court in respect to the many other matters in which such recourse serves the national interest. An all-or-nothing approach is not warranted by current U.S. foreign policy and does not reflect the range of American national interests.

Why Use the World Court?

The United States continues to have a considerable stake both in international law and in the World Court as to matters other than the exercise of its discretion to use armed force as a "last resort" in response to Communist encroachment. As noted, the United States participates in a large network of beneficial treaties, many of which commit it to a significant amount of judicial review under article 36(1) of the Statute of the International Court of Justice. The fact that law and the judicial process are inherently conservative coincides with the general U.S. interest in the development of principled, consistent, normative behavior, ranging from nonproliferation of nuclear weapons to the safeguarding of diplomats, suppression of terrorism, freedom of the seas and outer space, and protection of foreign investments. In these, and many other, areas the United States has more to lose by eliminating the judicial option than by nurturing it. Where relations with friendly states are concerned, it is to the U.S. advantage to promote judicial dispute settlement, particularly in instances when there is a favorable law-to-substance ratio. In relations with less friendly states, judicial proceedings may retard the escalation of disputes by allowing for a "cooling-off" period. The judicial option also is available to bring about reasonable solutions that cannot be achieved through negotiation because neither government can afford to be seen yielding to the other.

Since the judicial option has its uses, why not simply submit to the World Court the particular disputes in which such use is indicated? That could be done by specific agreement, applicable only to the single case, and would create no open-ended commitment to use the World Court in future situations. While this is certainly possible, such case-by-case submission negates one of the principal advantages of the system of adjudication, which is the development of the system itself. Consistent application of law is a major inducement to accepting a court's services. The knowledge that one is participating in an ongoing process—that the principles enunciated in case A will be applied by the court in some future case B—is an important consideration arguing in favor of participating at all. Absent that consistent application of the law, the argument for recourse to litigation is significantly weakened. If cases are brought before the World Court only by specific prior agreement of the disputing parties, that assurance of consistency is gone. (This is of particular concern with regard to the United States, where each agreement could be blocked by one-third plus one of the Senate.)

Another reason for continuing to use the World Court is the currently diminished, but still significant, vision of internationalism of a substantial sector of the American public. Every president, from Truman to Reagan, has proclaimed a "doctrine" implementing a particular version of the national interest and enunciating a strategy for dealing with communism. Beyond this preoccupation with the short-term tactics of East-West relations, there continues to exist a vision of world order, however dimly perceived, growing out of a historically rooted sense of overall evolutionary direction, of "where we want to go." Although the details of "world order models" are infinitely varied, each El Dorado must employ mechanisms for orderly dispute settlement. A radical step away from an already functioning, if imperfect, dispute settlement mechanism should not be taken—certainly not by the United States—except in defense of the most urgent national interest.

The Unilateralists' Arguments

No one who cherishes a vision of a peaceful world order can altogether dispense with the judicial option. At the same time, even a visionary must concede that the option entails, almost by definition, significant costs in the diminution of sovereignty. The commitment to settle a range of future disputes by recourse to adjudication—as opposed to the decision to submit one specific dispute-in-being to an ad hoc tribunal created expressly for that purpose by the disputants—involves a very considerable derogation from the sovereignty of a superpower. The U.S. investment in the judicial option must be determined by consideration of how much freedom of unilateral action it can give up without sacrificing essential short-term goals to contingent long-term aspirations. Surely, it is time for Americans to face that simple truth and to make a deliberate, carefully calibrated choice.

Unilateralists are undoubtedly right in contending that, in present circumstances, American recourse to military power—acting alone or in concert with close allies—remains critical for protecting the national self-interest, as well as for guarding world peace and holding the global line for democracy against aggressive totalitarian interests.

For example, if fighting were to break out between the Communist German Democratic Republic and our ally the German Federal Republic, then the North Atlantic Treaty would oblige the United States and its Western allies to respond to such an attack as if it were a direct assault on them all. That such aggression—or any other military thrust in Central Europe—has not occurred during the forty-year cold war is in part due to U.S. nuclear supremacy (in the early years) and parity with the Soviets (thereafter). As long as military deterrence is significant to maintaining peace between the Communist and democratic alliances, the finger on the trigger must be that of the United States, not those of judges from fifteen different legal systems from around the globe.

If fighting involving a U.S. ally were to break out, could the U.S. government justify deferring its decision to defend that ally until a majority of judges of a world court were satisfied by "proof" of who started what, whether the response was proportionate, and whether the methods of combat were within the legally permissible range of options? Even the United States Supreme Court has refused to tackle similar questions because they are too political. Whatever the World Court judges' considerable capabilities, they lack the power to stop a sovereign state—*any* sovereign state, probably—that has decided to resort to military force in what it perceives to be its national interest. War and peace will, and must continue to be, the responsibility of those capable of making them.

Most states, recognizing the powerlessness of the World Court in the face of military confrontation between states, have either refused to accept the jurisdiction of the court altogether or have excepted from its jurisdiction all situations of armed conflict. The history of the UN system clearly demonstrates that the only point in an actual military conflict when a court—or any other existing dispute-settlement machinery—plays a useful role is when the fighting has ended (to sort out legal liabilities) or when the parties are ready to lay down their arms and require a rationale that is politically acceptable to domestic constituents.

Had the United States continued—after the Nicaraguan case—to mortgage to an international judiciary its right to employ military deterrence, its government would have appeared either naively quixotic or baldly hypocritical. Worse, it would have sent a signal to friend and foe that the United States did not take seriously either its treaty commitments to the World Court or its treaty commitments to defend its allies. The peace of the world depends far more heavily on faith in treaty commitments than on faith in judicial settlement, not least because the latter rests on the former.

The United States, in sum, still needs the freedom to defend its freedom. It is imprudent for even the most enthusiastic admirers of global adjudication to argue otherwise.

The unilateralists also surely are correct in warning that the judges of the World Court are in a position to impose their personal visions of world order in accordance with their individual cultural biases. This is not to say that the judges would be biased. In practice, faced with invitations to make sweeping pronouncements in highly political situations, World Court judges often have sought narrow legal outcomes that divide costs and benefits more or less equally between litigants or that generate a relatively cost-free solution. The outcome of the Nicaraguan litigation's final (merits) phase demonstrates, however, that this is not invariably the case. When it comes to matters that are essential to the national interest it is not prudent to gamble, not even with reasonably good odds.

Compounding the problem, the unilateralists point out, is that the law is silent on many difficult issues. One of these issues is defining the right of states to use force in self-defense. For example, article 51 of the UN Charter permits "individual or collective self-defense" only against an actual "armed attack." Does that mean a nation must wait for the first nuclear bomb to land before it can launch a retaliatory strike? Must a tiny nation (Israel, for example) wait to be overrun before taking defensive military measures? If not, under what circumstances is "anticipatory self-defense" permissible? The task of resolving these issues cannot be left to the World Court judges, as it involves policy questions that can only be resolved—if at all—by negotiated agreement among sovereign states. If the world is not ready for world government, it is certainly not ready for a world government by fifteen jurists.

Nonetheless, the World Court has not acted in a way that should cause the United States to give up on it. Its judges realize that the World Court has, at most, a "fragile and precarious jurisdiction dependent on the continued consent of States." They know that to ignore that fact "would place the institution at great risk."[6] The unilateralists' arguments are valid to the extent that they urge caution in submitting matters of major importance to the World Court. The same arguments lose validity when they are used to conclude that it is never in the U.S. national interest to submit to any system of judicial settlement.

The Court We Need

But what kind of system of judicial settlement is in the U.S. national interest; and how does the existing system—the World Court—stack up against the ideal?

A stable international system—as opposed to a fragile, dangerous balance of terror—cannot be imagined, let alone built, without an institution of mandatory third-party dispute settlement. Courts are a necessary precondition of law. Even treaties, the most important (and most conservative) source of law, are of little use in the development of a stable international system if the parties are free to interpret their words any way they please. A system of laws governing at least some aspects of interstate relations that excludes the idea of third-party dispute settlement is unlikely to advance beyond a primitive balance-of-convenience level of socialization.

The necessary and desirable basic characteristics of the judicial instrument can be derived from its tasks and the environment in which they must be performed. In a world court, for example, the judges should be drawn from a cross section of legal systems. Only in this way would the court's opinions be widely acceptable to sovereign states and would the cultural and political biases of judges balance one another, creating an incentive for compromise and the search for consensus.

The court's jurisdiction should be applied and interpreted by its judges, not by disputing parties. A court that does not have the power to interpret its own jurisdiction is merely a panel of arbitrators, to be used when disputing parties feel like it, solving occasional disputes but creating no system of law. A judge from an "interested party" to a dispute should not sit in that case, or that judge's presence should be balanced by an ad hoc appointment to prevent unfair advantage.

The bench would have to consist of enough judges to give weight to opinions on complex, difficult issues. Those opinions would have to be carefully enunciated; based on reasoned, reciprocally applicable principles; and the outcome of a conscientious search for consensus.

Each of these characteristics is already, to a large extent, manifested by the present-day World Court. A blanket assertion of bias is not warranted by the record.[7] Its jurisprudence does not support a claim of bias. Its judges, who provide a reasonable cross section of the world's legal systems, are evidence of the proposition that there is often more in common between two judges, one of whom is a Western European (or Asian, African, or Latin American), than between two Western Europeans, one of whom is a judge. In the Libya-Malta case referred to earlier in this chapter, for example, both the Libyan and Maltese ad hoc judges voted with the majority. The U.S. and Canadian judges agreed in the case concerning the Gulf of Maine. In the key "merits" stage of the Iranian hostages case, the Polish judge voted "for" the United States while the Soviet judge did not. Bias is moderated by the tendency of judges to reach something approaching consensus and a realization that, if they fail, the decision—and the World Court itself—is weakened.

The court's jurisdiction, in practice, is closely circumscribed by its statute (although that statute, properly, reserves to the judges the task of interpreting the scope of their jurisdiction in actual cases[8]) and by the terms of states' acceptances of article 36(2) jurisdiction. Admittedly, the World Court has not yet evolved a doctrine—like the United States Supreme Court's "political question" doctrine—for staying out of disputes in which it is unlikely to be helpful. But the procedures for accepting the optional clause and article 36(2) compulsory jurisdiction leave each nation free to design these limitations itself. If the United States has not done so in the past, it is its own fault—a fault that it now has the opportunity to remedy.

The World Court is not the perfect instrument for an imperfect world. But if the United States is to retain a judicial option in the conduct of its foreign policy, the court it needs must resemble the one we have. Other, more specialized or regional, tribunals have a supplemental role, but it is in the national interest of the United States to encourage, rather than destroy, the only court with global reach.

The problem the United States has had with the World Court is not with the institution but with the way America has submitted to it—an ambiguous compromise between those who wanted a global supreme court and those who wanted nothing to do with it. The result was a policy marked by hypocrisy and self-deception, and the attainment of the worst of both worlds. To make matters worse, the United States failed to keep its legal strategy of adherence to the World Court in line with its evolving global political strategy.

What is now indicated is a return of the United States to acceptance of the general compulsory jurisdiction of the World Court under article 36(2), providing it is limited to disputes in which America's essential interests are not at stake. Such a new acceptance must specifically exempt from compulsory jurisdiction those disputes that the United States considers so critical to its national interest that it has demonstrated a willingness to use military force in order to prevail.

Preserving the Military Option

India accepted the compulsory jurisdiction of the World Court under article 36(2), but specifically excepted from that acceptance "disputes relating to or connected with facts or situations of hostilities, armed conflicts, individual or collective actions taken in self-defence, resistance to aggression, fulfillment of obligations imposed by international bodies, and other similar or related acts. . . ."[9] Israel, too, until November 21, 1985, when it joined the United States in terminating its adherence to article 36(2) jurisdiction, had excepted from the World Court's compulsory jurisdiction "disputes arising out of, or having reference to, any hostilities, war, state of war, breach of the peace, breach of armistice agreement or belligerent or military occupation . . . ."[10] Other such "military" exceptions are to be found in the acceptances of Kenya, Malawi, Malta, and El Salvador.[11]

A U.S. version of this qualification to the acceptance of the World Court's compulsory jurisdiction is suggested in Appendix B (Proposed Form of Qualified U.S. Acceptance of World Court Compulsory Jurisdiction). While the interpretation of this exception would be the prerogative of the World Court judges, there is no reason to believe that the court would not give effect to a clear limitation. Moreover, as this same reservation has been made by other states that accept article 36(2) jurisdiction, the World Court is unlikely to antagonize them all by ignoring, or misconstruing, it.

This is only the most obvious means of protecting essential U.S. interests while still promoting use of the World Court in appropriate circumstances. There are other ways in which the legitimate concerns of the unilateralists can be allayed while still accommodating a reasonable version of the multilateralist vision.

Using Chambers

There will be times when the United States will want a case to be decided by judges with special affinity for the issues, the law, or even the litigants. Although ordinarily the World Court sits as a full bench of fifteen judges (or more, if there are ad hoc appointees), the option of calling for a special chamber—composed of three or more judges—also is available. The formation of specialized chambers to hear certain kinds of disputes was incorporated into the Statute of the International Court of Justice in 1945.

In 1970, U.S. Secretary of State William P. Rogers proposed that the procedure be resuscitated to "relieve apprehension" on the part of potential litigants about submitting their disputes to the World Court.[12] By assuring the parties that they will be pleading before judges they respect and who are familiar with the issues, confidence in the process should be increased. In 1972, the World Court streamlined its rules to make chambers easier to use. The object, according to the then-World Court President Jiminez de Arechaga of Uruguay, was "to accord to the parties a decisive influence in the composition of ad hoc Chambers."[13] While, technically, the three or more judges making up a chamber are elected by the full bench of the World Court, Arechaga observed that "from a practical point of view, it is difficult to conceive that in normal circumstances those Members who have been suggested by the parties would not be elected" and that this reform was "a means of breathing new life into this dormant institution. . . ."[14]

Chambers established under the new rules have been employed in the Gulf of Maine case between the United States and Canada and in a boundary dispute between Mali and Upper Volta.[15] The United States and Italy have recently entered into an agreement to use the new procedures in a dispute concerning the Raytheon Company and Machlett Laboratories.[16]

Former State Department Legal Adviser Monroe Leigh has suggested that the United States could, consistent with the rules of the court, condition a new acceptance of the World Court's article 36(2) compulsory jurisdiction on the disputants agreeing to use a chamber, rather than the full bench.[17] In addition, the United States could make it clear that should the disputants' recommendations regarding the composition of a chamber be rejected—a situation that has not happened so far and is quite unlikely—the World Court's jurisdiction would fail (see Appendix B). Further, because there may be cases that the United States would prefer to put before the full bench, use of chambers should be an option open to either party, not a mandatory condition.

Implicit in such qualified acceptance of compulsory jurisdiction is the possibility that either party to a dispute could block recourse to the World Court by refusing to agree on the composition of a chamber. Although there is no reason to assume that the United States—or other countries—would use such a device, some further refinement could be introduced to avoid that potential problem. For example, the terms of the U.S. acceptance could specify procedures to be used in the event of a deadlock, such as having each party name one judge, or several, and having those judges name the neutral member.

Recourse to World Court chambers could be had by special agreement, without accepting article 36(2) compulsory jurisdiction—as in the U.S.-Canadian litigation concerning the Gulf of Maine. But such ad hoc recourse would vitiate the systemic benefits of adjudication. A further disadvantage is that any agreements concluded by the United States to use World Court chambers on an ad hoc basis would require the consent of two-thirds of the Senate, making the process extraordinarily difficult to invoke.

Requesting Elucidation (Not Implementation) of Legal Principles

In the litigation between Libya and Malta concerning their joint continental shelf, the disputants asked the World Court to decide "what principles and rules of international law are applicable" to the delimitation of the shelf but to leave it to the parties themselves to "delimit such areas by an agreement. . . ."[18] In other words, the World Court was asked to indicate the norms by which the parties, through negotiation, would resolve their conflict.

This was not the only time the World Court had been asked to render a decision limited to a declaration of law. In a dispute between Tunisia and Libya over their common boundary on the continental shelf, the disputing parties, through a special agreement, also assumed the task of applying the World Court's elucidation of legal principles to the actual situation.[19]

The benefit of restricting the World Court to pronouncements on the law is that it raises the law-to-substance ratio, allowing the judges to focus on the applicable general legal principles without having to dispose of the assets and interests involved.

The procedure creates an opportunity for nonlegal—for example, political or distributive—considerations to enter into, and perhaps modify, the application of the law in the particular instance without subverting the law. It also is possible that, in some instances, the World Court's intent is more likely to be implemented if the parties are given a share in shaping it.

While this limitation on World Court jurisdiction, so far, has been put in practice only by special agreement between particular disputing parties, there is no reason why a similar limitation could not be included as another part of any future U.S. acceptance of general article 36(2) compulsory jurisdiction. Anthony D'Amato, in a recent editorial in the *American Journal of International Law*, concludes that this would be in accordance with the Statute of the International Court of Justice.[20]

As with the use of chambers, this option should be available but not mandated by the terms of the U.S. acceptance. There probably will be circumstances in which the parties will consider it highly desirable—as in the Gulf of Maine case—to have the World Court not only enunciate the law but also apply it to the concrete facts. But in almost any dispute in which a judicial remedy might be useful, a decision limited to a finding of law—with the understanding that the parties themselves will negotiate in good faith to apply the law to the solution of the actual dispute—is preferable to no adjudication at all.

Symmetry and Continuity of Obligation

One of the complaints of the United States about the Nicaragua case is that it was forced into court on the basis of U.S. acceptance of article 36(2) compulsory jurisdiction by a country that had accepted that jurisdiction solely for the purposes of one particular litigation. If so, the United States had reason to resent the imbalance of obligations. The World Court held, however, that Nicaragua's acceptance of compulsory jurisdiction, though technically imperfect, had been in effect all along. Nonetheless, the United States should take steps to protect itself by insisting on strict symmetry—and continuity—of obligation between itself and other states with which it might at some future time engage in litigation.

In 1946, the United States Senate sought to ensure another kind of equality of obligation by tacking the Vandenberg reservation onto its acceptance of the World Court's compulsory jurisdiction. Under it, the Senate reserved the right of the United States not to go before the World Court in a dispute "arising under a multilateral treaty unless. . .all parties to the treaty affected by the decision are also parties" to the case.[21] In an era of multilateral treaties that, not infrequently, have a hundred or more parties, this provision is simply unrealistic.

It is also unnecessary. Although article 59 of the Statue of the International Court of Justice makes the World Court's decisions binding only on the parties before it in a particular case, a definitive interpretation of the World Court of the meaning of a treaty provision would undoubtedly be given due deference by other parties to the treaty. If such deference were not forthcoming, the United States would be justified in calling for renegotiation of the treaty or abrogating its adherence. The Vandenberg reservation, therefore, is not needed to achieve equality of obligation and protects nothing of essential interest to the United States that is not already protected by the statute and procedures of the World Court.

The British have taken care of the equality of obligation problem by declaring that jurisdiction shall not apply to disputes "in respect of which any other Party to the dispute has accepted the compulsory jurisdiction of the International Court of Justice only in relation to or for the purpose of the dispute; or where the acceptance of the Court's compulsory jurisdiction on behalf of any other Party to the dispute was deposited or ratified less than twelve months prior to the filing of the application bringing the dispute before the court."[22] The United States should include this same caveat in any future acceptance of the World Court's article 36(2) jurisdiction.

Summary: A Calibrated Response

The proposals for a carefully calibrated new acceptance of compulsory jurisdiction—examined here and illustrated in Appendix B—proceed on the assumption that the United States would not again accept the World Court's article 36(2) jurisdiction unless, this time around, it really means what it says. After judiciously balancing the national sovereignty costs against the global systemic benefits, the United States should make anew a carefully measured, deliberate but limited commitment to the World Court's article 36(2) compulsory jurisdiction.

This commitment naturally precludes any such self-judging provision as the former Connally reservation, which tried to have it both ways: to retain the absolute sovereignty of the United

States while obtaining the benefits of a significant global institution for resolving conflicts.

The logic of the course of action proposed here is based on a rejection of the extremes of both unilateralism and multilateralism. Absolute sovereignty and world government are both anachronistic pipedreams in a world of mixed interdependence and confrontation. The debate about a future U.S. relationship to the World Court should break away from the unrealistic expectation that either is a viable policy objective.

At the present stage of global socialization, the only assurance against wanton use of military force by a superpower is the political conscience of its citizenry. For now, a world court can neither augment nor substitute for that. Nevertheless, the United States cannot achieve total sovereignty, and to the extent that it must interact with the rest of the world, some of its interactions will be facilitated by having the judicial option available. It is possible to predict quite accurately which U.S. activities are likely to fall into this category and which are not.

The World Court is neither the only court we could imagine nor the only court operating between states. But no other court has its historic legacy, extensive jurisprudence, or broad base of participating states. The United States can and should learn to use the World Court to its advantage.

Notes

Chapter 1

1. *The Paquete Habana*, 175 U.S. 677 (1900).
2. UN Charter, arts. 92, 93.
3. UN Charter, art. 33(1).
4. UN Charter, art. 36(3).
5. UN Charter, art. 94(1).
6. UN Charter, art. 94(2).
7. *Corfu Channel case* (United Kingdom v. Albania), 1948 ICJ 15 (Judgment on preliminary objection).
8. Shabtai Rosenne, *The Law and Practice of the International Court* (2d rev. ed., 1985).
9. The Hague Convention No. 1 of 1907, art. 44. Statute of the International Court of Justice, arts. 4, 5.
10. Story related to author by Charles William Maynes, who served as assistant secretary of state for international organizations in the Carter administration.
11. Articles 4, 8, 10, 11, 12, supplemented by rules 40 and 61 of the Provisional Rules of Procedure of the Security Council and Rules 151 and 152 of the Rules of Procedure of the General Assembly.
12. For a detailed description of this procedure, and for even more complex arrangements operative in cases of deadlock, see Rosenne, *The Law and Practice of the International Court*, pp. 173-83.
13. G. A. Res. 1991 (XVIII) of 17 December 1963.
14. Statute of the International Court of Justice, art. 13(1).
15. Statute of the International Court of Justice, art. 13(3).
16. Statute of the International Court of Justice, art. 26; *Delimitation of the Maritime Boundary in the Gulf of Maine Area* (Canada v. United States), 1984 ICJ 246.
17. Statute of the International Court of Justice, art. 31.

18. For judicial examination of this concept of mutuality of obligation in complex practice, see *Right of Passage case* (India v. Port.), 1952 ICJ 125 (Preliminary objections). See also Rosenne, *The Law and Practice of the International Court*, pp. 313-18.

19. On the Soviet Union and France, see *Certain Expenses of the United Nations (Advisory Opinion)*, 1962 ICJ 151; on Morocco, see *Western Sahara (Advisory Opinion)*, 1975 ICJ 12.

Chapter 2

1. U.S. Department of State, *Instructions to the International (Peace) Conference at The Hague, 1899,* reprinted in J. Scott, *The Hague Peace Conference*, vol. 2, [Documents] 6, 8 (1909). See also U.S. Department of State, *1899 Foreign Relations of the United States*, pp. 511, 512 (1901). [Hereinafter (year) Foreign Relations U.S.]

2. Treaty of Amity, Commerce and Navigation, November 19, 1794, United States-Great Britain, 8 Stat. 116; T. S. No. 105.

3. Treaty of Washington, May 8, 1871, United States-Great Britain, 17 Stat. 863; T. S. No. 133.

4. *The New York Times*, September 16, 1872, p. 4, col. 4.

5. *The New York Times*, October 23, 1895, p. 4, col. 5.

6. *The New York Times*, April 20, 1890, p. 5, col. 1.

7. 1896 Foreign Relations U.S., p. 237 (1897).

8. *The New York Times*, January 13, 1897, p. 4, col. 2.

9. Ibid., col. 5.

10. J. Richardson, *Messages and Papers of the Presidents*, vol. 8, pp. 6236, 6242 (1911); *The New York Times*, March 5, 1897, p. 1, cols. 5-6.

11. The vote was forty-three in favor, twenty-six opposed. Fourteen nonvoting senators were reported paired. *Arbitration with Great Britain*, S. Doc. No. 161, 58th Cong., 3d sess., p. 33 (1897). [Confidential extracts from the *Executive Journal* of the Senate.]

12. Arbitration with Great Britain, "Senate Executive B" [Minority Report], March 18, 1897, *Reports of the Committee on Foreign Relations*, vol. 8, 1789-1901, S. Doc. 231, Pt. 8, 56th Cong., 2d sess., p. 412 (1901).

13. Ibid., pp. 413, 423.

14. American Bar Association, *Report of the Eighteenth Annual Meeting*, August 27, 28, 29 & 30, 1895, pp. 454-55 (1895).

15. New York State Bar Association, *Proceedings of the Nineteenth Annual Meeting with Reports for the Year 1895*, p. 291 (January 22 & 23, 1896, Albany, N. Y.) (1896).

16. Circular dated December 30, 1898, 1898 Foreign Relations U.S., pp. 551, 553 (1901).

17. U.S. Department of State, *Instructions to the International (Peace) Conference at The Hague, 1899*, [Documents] 6, 8 (1909) and Annex B, p. 15 (arts. 1, 3, 4, 5). See also 1899 Foreign Relations U.S., pp. 511, 512 (1901).

18. Convention for the Pacific Settlement of Disputes, July 29, 1899, art. 20, 32 Stat. 1779, T.S. No. 392, reprinted in *1899 Foreign Relations U.S.*, p. 521. Article 16 of the convention provides only: "arbitration is recognized by the Signatory Powers as the most effective, and at the same time most equitable, means of settling disputes which diplomacy has failed to settle."

19. Jeremy Bentham, "Legal Fictions" in *Works*, vol. VII, pp. 283-87, reproduced in C. K. Ogden, *Bentham's Theory of Fictions*, Appendix A, pp. 141-49 (1932).

20. Agreement for Arbitration of Certain Questions, October 14, 1903, Great Britain-France, 194 Consolidated Treaty Series, pp. 194, 195 (art. I) (C. Perry, ed., 1980); Arbitration Convention, November 1, 1904, United States-France, *Unperfected Treaties of the United States of America*, vol. 3, p. 475 (C. Wiktor, ed., 1977); Arbitration Convention, November 21, 1904, United States-Switzerland, idem, p. 479; Arbitration Convention, November 22, 1904, United States-Germany, idem, p. 483; Arbitration Convention, November 23, 1904, United States-Portugal, idem, p. 487; Arbitration Convention, December 12, 1904, United States-Great Britain, idem, p. 491; Arbitration Convention, December 14, 1904, United States-Italy, idem, p. 495; Arbitration Convention, December 31, 1904, United States-Spain, idem, p. 499; Arbitration Convention, January 6, 1905, United States-Austria-Hungary, *Unperfected Treaties of the United States of America*, vol. 4, p. 1 (C. Wiktor, ed., 1979); Arbitration Convention, January 18, 1905, United States-Mexico, idem, p. 5; Arbitration Convention, January 20, 1905, United States-Sweden and Norway, idem, p. 15; Arbitration Convention, February 11, 1905, United States-Japan, idem, p. 23.

21. Quoted in H. Cory, *Compulsory Arbitration of International Disputes*, p. 55 (1932). Cf. *The New York Times*, February 12, 1905, p. 1, col. 7.

22. *Instructions to the American Delegates to The Hague Conference*, 1907, in J. Scott, *The Hague Peace Conference*, vol. 2, [Documents] 181, 191 (1909) and in *1907 Foreign Relations in U.S.*, pp. 1128, 1135 (1910).

23. Arbitration Treaty, August 3, 1911, U.S.-France, *Unperfected*

Treaties of the United States of America, vol. 4, p. 217 (art. 1) (C. Wiktor, ed., 1979); Arbitration Treaty, August 3, 1911, U.S.-Great Britain, idem., p. 225 (art. 1).

24. *General Arbitration Treaties with Great Britain and France*, S. Doc. No. 98, 62d Cong., 1st sess., p. 4 (1911).

25. *General Arbitration Treaties with Great Britain and France*, S. Doc No. 476, 62d Cong., 2d sess., p. 9 (1911); 48 Cong. Rec., pp. 2954-55 (1912).

26. Protocol of Signature Relating to the Statute of the Permanent Court of International Justice, December 16, 1920, 6 L.N.T.S., pp. 380, 403 (art. 36) (1921).

27. *The New York Times*, October 31, 1922, p. 4, col. 2.

28. *The New York Times*, November 1, 1922, p. 1, col. 1.

29. 1923 Foreign Relations U.S., p. viii (1938).

30. 1930 *Public Papers of the President*, Herbert Hoover, pp. 560, 561 (1976).

31. *The New York Times*, January 17, 1935, p. 1, col. 4.

32. 79 Cong. Rec., p. 1147 (1935); *The New York Times*, January 30, 1935, p. 1, col. 6.

33. 79 Cong. Rec., p. 1146 (1935).

34. Ibid., p. 1132.

35. *The New York Times*, July 24, 1942, p. 4, col. 7.

36. U.S. Department of State, *Postwar Foreign Policy Preparation, 1939-1945*, pp. 114, 485-91 (1949).

37. Ibid., pp. 269, 595, 599.

38. See "Dumbarton Oaks Proposals for a General International Organization," chap. VII, UNCIO Docs., vol. 3, pp. 11-12, reprinted in U.S. Department of State, *The International Court of Justice: Selected Documents Related to the Drafting of the Statute*, p. 14 (1946).

39. UNCIO Docs., vol. 14, p. 37.

40. Ibid., pp. 146-61, 163-70, 224-29.

41. Harry S. Truman, *Memoirs*, vol. 1, p. 286 (1955).

42. UNCIO Docs., vol. 14, p. 164.

43. UNCIO Docs., vol. 13, p. 247.

44. Ibid., p. 559.

45. For Senate approval, see 91 Cong. Rec. 8190 (1945); for presidential ratification, see 15 Stat. 1031, T.S. No. 993 (1945).

46. See *Compulsory Jurisdiction, International Court of Justice: Hearings Before a Subcommittee of the Senate Committee on Foreign Relations on S. Res. 196*, 79th Cong., 2d sess., p. 133 (1946).

47. S. Rept. No. 1835, 79th Cong., 2d sess., pp. 2-3, 11 (1946).

48. 92 Cong. Rec., p. 10621 (1946).

49. Ibid., p. 10696.

50. Ibid., p. 10694.

51. Ibid., pp. 10684, 10691.

52. *Revision of the United Nations Charter: Hearings Before a Subcommittee of the Senate Committee on Foreign Relations,* 81st Cong., 2d sess., p. 366 (1950).

53. 92 Cong. Rec., pp. 10697, 10705-06 (1946).

54. *The New York Times,* August 27, 1946, p. 6, col. 1.

55. Manley O. Hudson, "The Arbitration Treaty with France," *American Journal of International Law,* Vol. 22, pp. 368-69 (1928).

56. *The New York Times,* December 11, 1959, p. 15, cols. 4-5.

57. *The New York Times,* September 3, 1958, p. 1, col. 3.

58. *Interhandel Case* (Switzerland v. United States), 1959 ICJ 4, 24-25 (Judgment on preliminary objections).

59. *The New York Times,* April 9, 1984, p. A1, col. 2; Department of State Bulletin, vol. 84, no. 2087, p. 89 (June 1984).

60. U.S. Department of State, *Statement: U.S. Withdrawal from the Proceedings Initiated by Nicaragua in the International Court of Justice,* International Legal Materials, vol. XXIV, p. 246 (1985).

61. Ibid., pp. 246-48.

62. Lecture by Allan Gerson, "Should the U.S. Rethink its Attitude toward the World Court? Implications of the Dispute with Nicaragua on American Foreign Policy," John Bassett Moore Society of International Law, University of Virginia School of Law, November 17, 1984 (mimeo). See also Thomas M. Franck, "Icy Day at the ICJ," *American Journal of International Law,* Vol. 79, p. 379-80 (1985).

63. These are found in the declarations of Liberia, Malawi, Mexico, the Philippines, and the Sudan. See *1983-84 International Court of Justice Yearbook,* pp. 73, 75, 79, 84, 86 (1984).

Chapter 3

1. Department of State press statement, October 7, 1985.

2. U.S. Department of State, "Talking Points: Compulsory Jurisdiction of the ICJ," October 7, 1985, p. 2 (mimeo).

3. Fred L. Morrison, "Treaties as a Source of Jurisdiction for the International Court of Justice with Special Reference to the Practice of the United States of America," draft presented to a research group of the American Society of International Law, 1986 (mimeo).

4. Ibid.

5. Economic Cooperation with Austria, 1948, 62 Stat. 2137, T.I.A.S. No. 1780.

6. E.g., Treaty of Friendship, Establishment and Navigation between the United States of America and The Kingdom of Belgium, 1961, 14 U.S.T. 1284, T.I.A.S. No. 5432.

7. See *Nicaragua v. United States*, 1984 ICJ 392; *United States Diplomatic and Consular Staff in Tehran* (United States v. Iran), 1980 ICJ 3.

8. Consular Convention with Belgium, 1969, 25 U.S.T. 41, T.I.A.S. No. 7775, art. 46. Consular Convention with Republic of Korea, 1963, 14 U.S.T. 1637, T.I.A.S. No. 5469, art. 16. Columbia River Basin Treaty with Canada, 1961, 15 U.S.T. No. 1555, T.I.A.S. No. 5638, art. 16.

9. Morrison, "Treaties as a Source of Jurisdiction," pp. 17-22.

10. On the law of the sea, see Convention on the Territorial Sea and the Contiguous Zone, 15 U.S.T. 1606, T.I.A.S. No. 5639, 516 U.N.T.S. 205; Convention on the High Seas, 13 U.S.T. 2313, T.I.A.S. No. 5200, 450 U.N.T.S. 82; Convention on the Continental Shelf, 15 U.S.T. 471, T.I.A.S. No. 5578, 499 U.N.T.S. 311; Convention on Fishing and Conservation of the Living Resource of the High Seas, 559 U.N.T.S. 285; Optional Protocol of Signature Concerning the Compulsory Settlement of Disputes, 450 U.N.T.S. 169. On narcotic drugs see 48 Stat. 1543, T.S. No. 863; 61 Stat. 2230, T.S. No. 1671; 62 Stat. 1796, T.I.A.S. No. 1859 (1931, 1951). On copyright, see 6 U.S.T. 2731, T.I.A.S. No. 3324 (1952); 25 U.S.T. 1341, T.I.A.S. No. 7868 (1971).

11. The Genocide Convention, 78 U.N.T.S. 1021, art. 9.

12. Morrison, "Treaties as a Source of Jurisdiction," p. 19.

13. For the Food and Agriculture Organization, see 60 Stat. 1886, T.I.A.S. No. 1554 (1945); 12 U.S.T. 980, T.I.A.S. No. 4803 (1959). For the International Labor Organization, see 62 Stat. 3485, T.I.A.S. No. 1868 (1946). For the International Atomic Energy Agency, see 8 U.S.T. 1093, T.I.A.S. No. 3873 (1956). For the International Civil Aviation Organization, see 61 Stat. 1180, T.I.A.S. No. 1591 (1944). For the World Health Organization, see 62 Stat. 2679, T.I.A.S. No. 1808 (1946).

14. Morrison, "Treaties as a Source of Jurisdiction," p. 22.

15. Ibid., Table 2, p. 23.

16. Ibid., p. 35.

17. Ibid., p. 37.

Chapter 4

1. Thomas M. Franck, *Nation against Nation: What Became of the United Nations Dream and What the U.S. Can Do About It*, pp. 9-15 (1985).

2. Proceedings of the 1984 annual meeting of the American Society of International Law (forthcoming, 1986).

3. Monroe Leigh, memorandum on "The Evolution of Attitudes Towards the World Court" to the Panel on the International Court of Justice of the American Society of International Law, 1985, p. 5 (mimeo).

4. Ibid., p. 6.

5. Ibid., pp. 6-7.

6. *Anglo-Iranian Oil Co. Case* (United Kingdom v. Iran), 1952 ICJ 93 at 161 (Preliminary objection) (Judge Carneiro dissenting).

7. For the first decision, see *United States Diplomatic and Consular Staff in Tehran* (United States v. Iran), 1979 ICJ 7 (Provisional measures, Order of 15 December 1979). For the second decision, see *United States Diplomatic and Consular Staff in Tehran* (United States v. Iran), 1980 ICJ 3.

8. *Baker v. Carr*, 369 U.S. 186 at 267 (1962) (Justice Frankfurter dissenting).

9. *Certain Expenses of the United Nations (Advisory Opinion)*, 1962 ICJ 151 at 254.

10. Department of State, press statement, October 7, 1985, p. 2.

11. "Reflections of the State Department on the U.S. and the World Court," *World Affairs*, Vol. 148, p. 58 (1985).

12. Eugene V. Rostow, memorandum to the Panel on the International Court of Justice of the American Society of International Law, October 4, 1985, p. 9 (mimeo).

13. Shabtai Rosenne, *The Law and Practice of the International Court* (2d rev. ed., 1985), pp. 2-3.

14. Sir Hersch Lauterpacht, *The Function of Law in the International Community*, pp. 5, 153, 155 (1933).

15. Hans Morgenthau, *Policies Among Nations*, p. 344 (1953).

16. *United States Diplomatic and Consular Staff in Tehran* (United States v. Iran), 1980 ICJ 3.

17. See Summary of Argument by Professor Louis B. Sohn, Verbatim Record, Public Sitting held on October 16, 1984, ICJ Doc. CR 84/18, p. 67.

18. Bruce Rashkow, "Fact Finding by the World Court," *World Affairs*, Vol. 148, p. 50 (1985).

19. *Nicaragua v. United States of America,* 1984 ICJ Pleadings, Counter-Memorial submitted by the United States (The Question of the Jurisdiction of the Court to Entertain the Dispute and of the Admissibility of Nicaragua's Application), p. 224.

20. Rashkow, "Fact Finding by the World Court," p. 50.

21. Ibid, p. 51.

22. Ibid.

23. Keith Highet, memorandum on "Evidence in the International Court" to the Panel on the International Court of Justice of the American Society of International Law, April 16, 1986, p. 8, n. 23.

24. See Statute of the International Court of Justice, arts. 44, 49, 50, 52, and rule 66 of the Court's Rules of Procedure.

25. Rosenne, *The Law and Practice of the International Court,* p. 580.

26. Statute of the International Court of Justice, art. 53(2).

27. See Rule 69, para. 2 of the Court's Rules of Procedure.

28. Sir Hersch Lauterpacht, *The Development of International Law by the International Court,* p. 48 (1958).

29. *Western Sahara (Advisory Opinion),* 1975 ICJ 12.

30. *Delimitation of the Czechosolovak-Polish Frontier,* 1923 PCIJ, Ser. B, No. 8; *The Monastery of Saint-Naoum* (Albanian Frontier), 1924 PCIJ, Ser. B, No. 9; *Legal Status of Eastern Greenland* (Denmark v. Norway), 1933 PCIJ, Ser. A/B, No. 53; *Sovereignty over Certain Frontier Land* (Belgium v. Netherlands), 1959 ICJ 209; *Minquiers and Ecrehos* (France v. United Kingdom), 1953 ICJ 47; *Temple of Preah Vihar* (Cambodia v. Thailand) (Merits), 1962 ICJ 6; *North Sea Continental Shelf,* 1969 ICJ 3; *Case Concerning the Continental Shelf* (Tunisia/Libyan Arab Jamahiriya), 1982 ICJ 18; *Delimitation of the Maritime Boundary in the Gulf of Maine Area* (Canada/United States), 1984 ICJ 246. See also *Case Concerning the Continental Shelf* (Libyan Arab Jamahiriya/Malta), 1985 ICJ 13.

31. Highet, memorandum on "Evidence in the International Court," p. 22.

32. Experts' Report of January 8, 1949, ICJ 142-51.

33. John Norton Moore, on behalf of the United States, argued during the Nicaraguan litigation that a factual finding by the World Court "would be of no value except, perhaps, for a discrete moment in time 'frozen' by the Court on the basis of the evidence then available to it." *Verbatim Record* of the hearing of October 16, 1984, C.R. 84/19, p. 76.

34. Testimony on cross-examination of David MacMichael, the lead witness for Nicaragua and a former CIA employee. See Verbatim Record, ICJ, *Nicaragua v. United States,* September 16, 1985, C.R. 85/21. Also quoted in John Norton Moore, "The Secret War in Central America and the Future of World Order," *American Journal of International Law,* Vol. 80, pp. 66-69 (1986).

35. Ibid.

36. *United States Diplomatic and Consular Staff in Tehran* (United States v. Iran), 1980 ICJ 3 at 9-10.

37. Highet, memorandum on "Evidence in the International Court," p. 46.

38. Allan Gerson, "Why Bow to the World Court When Few Others Do?" *World Affairs,* Vol. 148, p. 6 (1985).

39. Department of State, press statement, October 7, 1985.

40. Rosenne, *The Law and Practice of the International Court,* p. 419.

41. Leo Gross, memorandum on "Compulsory Jurisdiction" to the Panel on the International Court of Justice of the American Society of International Law, November 6, 1985, p. 7.

42. See J. B. Elkind, *Non-Appearance Before the International Court of Justice,* espec. pp. 38-41 (1984).

43. *The Nottebohm Case* (Liechtenstein v. Guatemala), 1953 ICJ 111; Second Phase, 1955 ICJ 4.

44. *The Asylum Case* (Colombia v. Peru), 1950 ICJ 266. See Elkind, *Non-Appearance Before the International Court of Justice,* p. 199.

45. *Nuclear Test Cases* (New Zealand v. France), 1974 ICJ 457; (Australia v. France), 1974 ICJ 253.

46. *The Aegean Sea Continental Shelf Case* (Greece v. Turkey), 1978 ICJ 3.

47. 1 U.N.T.S. 3; 211 U.N.T.S. 109; 219 U.N.T.S. 179; 265 U.N.T.S. 221; 316 U.N.T.S. 59; 482 U.N.T.S. 187; 654 U.N.T.S. 335.

48. Letter to the secretary-general from Ambassador Stephen Lewis, September 10, 1985.

49. *1983-84 International Court of Justice Yearbook,* pp. 57-91.

Chapter 5

1. Richard B. Bilder, "International Dispute Settlement and the Role of Adjudication," Panel on the International Court of Justice of the American Society of International Law, Draft Rev. 1, January 26, 1986.

2. See excellent discussion in Oscar Schachter, "The Right of States to Use Armed Force," *Michigan Law Review*, Vol. 82, pp. 1642-43 (1984).

3. Oscar Schachter, "In Defense of International Rules on the Use of Force," *University of Chicago Law Review*, Vol. 53, p. 137 (1986).

4. Derek Bowett, "The Interrelation of Theories of Intervention and Self-Defense," in J. N. Moore, ed., *Law and Civil War in the Modern World*, pp. 41-46 (1974).

5. See Thomas M. Franck and Edward Weisband, *World Politics: Verbal Strategy Among the Superpowers*, pp. 33-48 (1971).

6. Ibid., pp. 40-48.

7. Address by Ambassador Jeane J. Kirkpatrick, National Press Club, Washington, D.C., May 30, 1984.

Chapter 6

1. *Case Concerning the Continental Shelf* (Libyan Arab Jamahiriya/Malta), 1985 ICJ 13.

2. Ibid., pp. 39-41.

3. Presidential Proclamation No. 2667, September 28, 1945, 10 Fed. Reg. 12303 (1945).

4. Charles Krauthammer, "The Poverty of Realism," *The New Republic*, February 17, 1986, pp. 15-16.

5. Ibid., p. 14.

6. Oscar Schachter, *International Law in Theory and Practice, General Court in Public International Law, Recueil des Cours*, Vol. 178, p. 67 (1982).

7. Between 1945 and 1985, the U.S. member of the World Court voted with the majority in forty-three instances involving adversary proceedings and thirteen instances involving advisory opinions. The U.S. judge differed from the majority in only seven decisions and in four issues pertaining to advisory opinions.

8. Statute of the International Court of Justice, article 31(2), (3).

9. Declarations Recognizing Jurisdiction, 1983-84 ICJ Yearbook, p. 69 (India).

10. Ibid., p. 70 (Israel).

11. Ibid., pp. 72-73 (Kenya), p. 75 (Malawi), p. 76 (Malta), and pp. 65-66 (El Salvador).

12. Address by William P. Rogers, The American Society of International Law, 1970 Proc. American Society of International Law, p. 288.

13. Jiminez de Arechaga, "The Amendments to the Rules of Procedure of the International Court of Justice," *American Journal of International Law*, Vol. 67, p. 2 (1973).

14. Ibid., pp. 2-3.

15. For the Gulf of Maine case, see *Maritime Boundary Treaty*, United States and Canada, March 29, 1979, T.I.A.S. No. 10204; *Delimitation of the Maritime Boundary in the Gulf of Maine Area* (Canada v. United States), 1984 ICJ 246. For the boundary dispute between Mali and Upper Volta, see Special Agreement Between Mali and Upper Volta, September 16, 1983, reprinted in *International Legal Materials*, Vol. XXII, p. 1252 (1983).

16. U.S. Department of State, Statement on U.S.-Italy Submission of Raytheon/Machlett Dispute to World Court (1985) (mimeo).

17. Monroe Leigh, memorandum on "The Use of Special Chambers" to the Panel on the International Court of Justice of the American Society of International Law, September 26, 1985, p. 14.

18. *Case Concerning the Continental Shelf*, p. 16 (arts. 1 and 3 of the Special Agreement Between Libya and Malta).

19. *Case Concerning the Continental Shelf* (Tunisia/Libyan Arab Jamahiriya), 1982 ICJ 18.

20. Anthony D'Amato, "The United States Should Accept, By a New Declaration, The General Compulsory Jurisdiction of the World Court," *American Journal of International Law*, Vol. 80, p. 335 (1986).

21. Declarations Recognizing Jurisdiction, p. 91 (United States).

22. Ibid., p. 90 (United Kingdom).

Appendixes

Appendix A

VOTING RECORD OF U.S. MEMBER OF THE WORLD COURT (1945-85)

CASE/PHASE	JUDGMENT/ ORDER	U.S. MEMBER	PROCEEDING	DISSENTED	VOTED WITH MAJORITY
The Corfu Channel Case (People's Republic of Albania v. United Kingdom)/ Preliminary objection to admissibility and jurisdiction	Judgment of 25 March 1948	Green H. Hackworth	Adversary		X
Conditions of Admission of a State to Membership in the United Nations (Article 4 of the Charter)	Advisory Opinion of 28 May 1948	Hackworth	Advisory		X
The Corfu Channel Case/ Questions to be put to the Committee of Experts	Order of 17 December 1948	Hackworth	Adversary		X
The Corfu Channel Case/Merits	Judgment of 9 April 1949	Hackworth	Adversary		X
Reparation for Injuries Suffered in the Service of the United Nations	Advisory Opinion of 11 April 1949	Hackworth	Advisory	X	

The Corfu Channel Case/Experts' role in the assessment of the amount of compensation	Order of 19 November 1949	Hackworth	Adversary	X
Competence of the General Assembly for the Admission of New Members to the United Nations/Request for advisory opinion	Order of 2 December 1949	Hackworth	Advisory	X
The Corfu Channel Case/Assessment of the amount of compensation due	Judgment of 15 December 1949	Hackworth	Adversary	X
Competence of the General Assembly for the Admission of a State to the United Nations	Advisory Opinion of 3 March 1950	Hackworth	Advisory	X
Interpretation of Peace Treaties with Bulgaria, Hungary, and Romania	Advisory Opinion of 30 March 1950	Hackworth	Advisory	X
International Status of South-West Africa	Advisory Opinion of 11 July 1950	Hackworth	Advisory	X

Appendix A (continued)

VOTING RECORD OF U.S. MEMBER OF THE WORLD COURT (1945-85)

CASE/PHASE	JUDGMENT/ORDER	U.S. MEMBER	PROCEEDING	DISSENTED	VOTED WITH MAJORITY
Interpretation of Peace Treaties with Bulgaria, Hungary, and Romania/Second phase	Advisory Opinion of 18 July 1950	Hackworth	Advisory		X
Colombian-Peruvian Asylum Case	Judgment of 20 November 1950	Hackworth	Adversary		X
Case Concerning Rights of Nationals of the United States of America in Morocco (France/United States of America)/Application	Order of 22 November 1950	Hackworth	Adversary		X
Request for Interpretation of the Judgment of 20 November 1950 in the Colombian-Peruvian Asylum Case	Judgment of 27 November 1950	Hackworth	Adversary		X
Ambatielos Case (Greece/United Kingdom)/Application	Order of 18 May 1951	Hackworth	Adversary		X

Case	Date	Judge	Type		
Reservations to the Convention on the Prevention and Punishment of the Crime of Genocide	Advisory Opinion of 28 May 1951	Hackworth	Advisory	X	
Haya de la Torre Case (Colombia/Peru)	Judgment of 13 June 1951	Hackworth	Adversary	X	
Anglo-Iranian Oil Co. Case (United Kingdom/Iran)/Request for the indication of interim measures of protection	Order of 5 July 1951	Hackworth	Adversary	X	
Anglo-Iranian Oil Co. Case/Application	Order of 5 July 1951	Hackworth	Adversary	X	
Fisheries Case (United Kingdom v. Norway)	Judgment of 18 December 1951	Hackworth	Adversary	concurring declaration	
Ambatielos Case/Preliminary objections regarding jurisdiction and arbitration	Judgment of 1 July 1952	Hackworth	Adversary	X	
Anglo-Iranian Oil Co. Case/Preliminary objection to jurisdiction	Judgment of 22 July 1952	Hackworth	Adversary		X

Appendix A (continued)

VOTING RECORD OF U.S. MEMBER OF THE WORLD COURT (1945-85)

CASE/PHASE	JUDGMENT/ ORDER	U.S. MEMBER	PROCEEDING	DISSENTED	VOTED WITH MAJORITY
Case Concerning Rights of Nationals of the United States of America in Morocco	Judgment of 27 August 1952	Hackworth	Adversary	joined common statement of dissenting opinion	
Ambatielos Case/Merits: obligation to arbitrate	Judgment of 19 May 1953	Hackworth	Adversary		X
"Electricite de Beyrouth" Company Case (France v. Lebanon)/ Application	Order of 20 October 1953	Hackworth	Adversary		X
The Minquiers and Ecrehos Case (France/United Kingdom)	Judgment of 17 November 1953	Hackworth	Adversary		X
Nottebohm Case (Liechtenstein v. Guatemala)/Preliminary objection to jurisdiction	Judgment of 18 November 1953	Hackworth	Adversary		X
Effect of Awards of Compensation Made by the UN Administrative Tribunal	Advisory Opinion of 13 June 1954	Hackworth	Advisory	X	

Case				
Case of the Monetary Gold Removed from Rome in 1943 (Italy v. France, United Kindgom)/Preliminary question of jurisdiction	Judgment of 15 June 1954	Hackworth	Adversary	X
Treatment in Hungary of Aircraft and Crew of United States of America (United States of America v. Hungarian People's Republic)/Submission to jurisdiction	Order of 12 July 1954	Hackworth	Adversary	X
Treatment in Hungary of Aircraft and Crew of United States of America (United States of America v. Union of Soviet Socialist Republics)/Submission to jurisdiction	Order of 12 July 1954	Hackworth	Adversary	X
Nottebohm Case/Second phase	Judgment of 6 April 1955	Hackworth	Adversary	X
Voting Procedure on Questions Relating to Reports and Petitions Concerning the Territory of South-West Africa	Advisory Opinion of 7 June 1955	Hackworth	Advisory	X
Case Concerning Rights of Passage Over Indian Territory (Portugal v. India/Application	Order of 13 March 1956	Hackworth	Adversary	X

Appendix A (continued)

VOTING RECORD OF U.S. MEMBER OF THE WORLD COURT (1945-85)

CASE/PHASE	JUDGMENT/ ORDER	U.S. MEMBER	PROCEEDING	DISSENTED	VOTED WITH MAJORITY
Aerial Incident of 10 March 1953 (United States of America v. Czechoslovakia)/Submission to jurisdiction	Order of 14 March 1956	Hackworth	Adversary		X
Aerial Incident of 7 October 1952 (United States of America v. Union of Soviet Socialist Republics)/Submission to jurisdiction	Order of 14 March 1956	Hackworth	Adversary		X
Antarctica Case (United Kingdom v. Argentina)/Submission to jurisdiction	Order of 16 March 1956	Hackworth	Adversary		X
Antarctica Case (United Kingdom v. Chile)/Submission to jurisdiction	Order of 16 March 1956	Hackworth	Adversary		X
Admissibility of Hearings of Petitioners by the Committee on South-West Africa	Advisory Opinion of 1 June 1956	Hackworth	Advisory		X
Judgments of the Administrative Tribunal of the ILO upon Complaints Made Against UNESCO	Advisory Opinion of 23 October 1956	Hackworth	Advisory	X	

Case	Date	Judge	Type	Notes
Case of Certain Norwegian Loans (France v. Norway)	Judgment of 6 July 1957	Hackworth	Adversary	X
Interhandel Case (Switzerland v. United States of America/Request for the indication of interim measures of protection	Order of 24 October 1957	Hackworth	Adversary	concurs in separate opinion written by Judge Klaestad
Case Concerning Right of Passage over Indian Territory/Preliminary objections to jurisdiction	Judgment of 26 November 1957	Hackworth	Adversary	X
Case Concerning Aerial Incident of 27 July 1955 (Israel v. Bulgaria)/Application	Order of 26 November 1957	Hackworth	Adversary	X
Case Concerning Aerial Incident of 27 July 1955 (United States of America v. Bulgaria)/Application	Order of 26 November 1957	Hackworth	Adversary	X
Case Concerning Aerial Incident of 27 July 1955 (United Kingdom v. Bulgaria)/Application	Order of 26 November 1957	Hackworth	Adversary	X
Case Concerning the Barcelona Traction, Light and Power Company, Limited (Belgium v. Spain)/Application	Order of 18 October 1958	Hackworth	Adversary	X

Appendix A (continued)

VOTING RECORD OF U.S. MEMBER OF THE WORLD COURT (1945-85)

CASE/PHASE	JUDGMENT/ORDER	U.S. MEMBER	PROCEEDING	DISSENTED	VOTED WITH MAJORITY
Case Concerning the Application of the Convention of 1902 governing the Guardianship of Infants (Netherlands v. Sweden)	Judgment of 28 November 1958	Hackworth	Adversary		X
Case Concerning Aerial Incident of 4 September 1954 (United States of America v. Union of Soviet Socialist Republics)/Submission to jurisdiction	Order of 9 December 1958	Hackworth	Adversary		X
Interhandel Case (Switzerland v. United States of America)/Preliminary objections to jurisdiction	Judgment of 21 March 1959	Hackworth	Adversary		separate opinion
Case Concerning Aerial Incident of 27 July 1955 (Israel v. Bulgaria)/Preliminary objections to jurisdiction	Judgment of 26 May 1959	Hackworth	Adversary		X
*Case Concerning Sovereignty over Certain Frontier Land (Belgium/Netherlands)	Judgment of 20 June 1959	Hackworth	Adversary		

Case	Date	Judge	Type	
Case Concerning the "Compagnie du Port, des Quais et des Entrepots de Beyrouth" and the "Societe Radio-Orient" (France v. Lebanon)/Application	Order of 18 June 1959	Hackworth	Adversary	X
Case Concerning Aerial Incident of 7 November 1954/Submission to jurisdiction	Order of 7 October 1959	Hackworth	Adversary	X
Case Concerning Right of Passage over Indian Territory/Merits	Judgment of 12 April 1960	Hackworth	Adversary	X
*Constitution of the Maritime Safety Committee of the Inter-Governmental Maritime Consultative Organization	Advisory Opinion of 8 June 1960	Hackworth	Advisory	
Case Concerning the Arbitral Award Made by the King of Spain on 23 December 1906 (Honduras v. Nicaragua)	Judgment of 18 November 1960	Hackworth	Adversary	X
**Case Concerning the Temple of Preah Vihear (Cambodia v. Thailand)/Preliminary objections to jurisdiction	Judgment of 26 May 1961	U.S. judge not present	Adversary	
**Case Concerning the Temple of Preah Vihear/Merits	Judgment of 15 June 1962	U.S. judge not present	Adversary	

Appendix A (continued)

VOTING RECORD OF U.S. MEMBER OF THE WORLD COURT (1945-85)

CASE/PHASE	JUDGMENT/ ORDER	U.S. MEMBER	PROCEEDING	DISSENTED	VOTED WITH MAJORITY
Certain Expenses of the United Nations (Article 17, Paragraph 2, of the Charter)	Advisory Opinion of 20 July 1962	Philip C. Jessup	Advisory		X
South-West Africa Cases (Ethiopia v. South Africa; Liberia v. South Africa)/Preliminary objections to existence of dispute and jurisdiction	Judgment of 21 December 1962	Jessup	Adversary		separate opinion
Case Concerning the Northern Cameroons (Cameroon v. United Kingdom)/Preliminary objections as to existence of dispute and jurisdiction	Judgment of 2 December 1963	Jessup	Adversary		separate declaration
Case Concerning the Barcelona Traction, Light and Power Company, Limited/Preliminary objections to jurisdiction and admissibility of claim	Judgment of 24 July 1964	Jessup	Adversary		separate declaration

*South-West Africa Cases, (Ethiopia v. South Africa; Liberia v. South Africa)/Composition of the court	Order of 18 March 1965	Jessup	Adversary		
*South-West Africa Cases/Inspection in loco	Order of 29 November 1965	Jessup	Adversary		
South-West Africa Cases/Second phase	Judgment of 18 July 1966	Jessup	Adversary	X	
North Sea Continental Shelf Cases (Federal Republic of Germany/Denmark; Federal Republic of Germany/Netherlands)	Judgment of 20 February 1969	Jessup	Adversary		separate opinion
Case Concerning the Barcelona Traction, Light and Power Company, Limited/Second phase	Judgment of 5 February 1970	Jessup	Adversary		separate opinion
Legal Consequences for States of the Continued Presence of South Africa in Namibia (South-West Africa) Notwithstanding Security Council Resolution 276 (1970)/Request for advisory opinion: objection to the composition of the court	Order No. 1 of 26 January 1971	Hardy Cross Dillard	Advisory		X

Appendix A (continued)

VOTING RECORD OF U.S. MEMBER OF THE WORLD COURT (1945-85)

CASE/PHASE	JUDGMENT/ ORDER	U.S. MEMBER	PROCEEDING	DISSENTED	VOTED WITH MAJORITY
Legal Consequences for States of the Continued Presence of South Africa in Namibia/ Request for advisory opinion: objection to the composition of the court	Order No. 2 of 26 January 1971	Dillard	Advisory		X
*Legal Consequences for States of the Continued Presence of South Africa in Namibia/ Request for advisory opinion: objection to the composition of the court	Order No. 3 of 26 January 1971	Dillard	Advisory		
Legal Consequences for States of the Continued Presence of South Africa in Namibia/ Request for advisory opinion: request for judge ad hoc	Order of 29 January 1971	Dillard	Advisory	X	
Legal Consequences for States of the Continued Presence of South Africa in Namibia	Advisory Opinion of 21 June 1971	Dillard	Advisory		separate opinion

Application for Review of Judgment No. 158 of the United Nations Administrative Tribunal/Request for advisory opinion	Order of 14 July 1972	Dillard	Advisory	X
Fisheries Jurisdiction Case (United Kingdom v. Iceland)/Request for the indication of interim measures of protection	Order of 17 August 1972	Dillard	Adversary	X
Fisheries Jurisdiction Case (Federal Republic of Germany v. Iceland)/Request for the indication of interim measures of protection	Order of 17 August 1972	Dillard	Adversary	X
Appeal Relating to the Jurisdiction of the ICAO Council (India v. Pakistan)	Judgment of 18 August 1972	Dillard	Adversary	separate opinion
*Fisheries Jurisdiction Case (United Kingdom v. Iceland)/Order of pleadings	Order of 18 August 1972	Dillard	Adversary	
*Fisheries Jurisdiction Case (Federal Republic of Germany v. Iceland)/Order of pleadings	Order of 18 August 1972	Dillard	Adversary	

Appendix A (continued)

VOTING RECORD OF U.S. MEMBER OF THE WORLD COURT (1945-85)

CASE/PHASE	JUDGMENT/ ORDER	U.S. MEMBER	PROCEEDING	DISSENTED	VOTED WITH MAJORITY
Fisheries Jurisdiction Case (United Kingdom v. Iceland)/ Jurisdiction of the court	Judgment of 2 February 1973	Dillard	Adversary		X
Fisheries Jurisdiction Case (Federal Republic of Germany v. Iceland)/Jurisdiction of the court	Judgment of 2 February 1973	Dillard	Adversary		X
**Nuclear Tests Case (Australia v. France)/Request for the indication of interim measures of protection	Order of 22 June 1973	U.S. judge not present	Adversary		
**Nuclear Tests Case (New Zealand v. France)/Request for the indication of interim measures of protection	Order of 22 June 1973	U.S. judge not present	Adversary		
Application for Review of Judgment No. 158 of the United Nations Administrative Tribunal	Advisory Opinion of 12 July 1973	Dillard	Advisory		separate opinion

Case	Order/Judgment	U.S. judge		
**Fisheries Jurisdiction Case (United Kingdom v. Iceland)/Continuance of interim measures of protection	Order of 12 July 1973	U.S. judge not present	Adversary	
**Fisheries Jurisdiction Case (Federal Republic of Germany v. Iceland)/Continuance of interim measures of protection	Order of 12 July 1973	U.S. judge not present	Adversary	
*Nuclear Tests Case (Australia v. France)/Application by Fiji for permission to intervene	Order of 12 July 1973	U.S. judge not present	Adversary	
**Nuclear Tests Case (New Zealand v. France)/Application by Fiji for permission to intervene	Order of 12 July 1973	U.S. judge not present	Adversary	
**Case Concerning Trial of Pakistani Prisoners of War (Pakistan v. India)/Request for the indication of interim measures of protection	Order of 13 July 1973	U.S. judge not present	Adversary	
Fisheries Jurisdiction Case (United Kingdom v. Iceland)/Merits	Judgment of 25 July 1974	Dillard	Adversary	separate opinion
Fisheries Jurisdiction Case (Federal Republic of Germany v. Iceland)/Merits	Judgment of 25 July 1974	Dillard	Adversary	separate declaration

Appendix A (continued)

VOTING RECORD OF U.S. MEMBER OF THE WORLD COURT (1945-85)

CASE/PHASE	JUDGMENT/ORDER	U.S. MEMBER	PROCEEDING	DISSENTED	VOTED WITH MAJORITY
Nuclear Tests Case (Australia v. France)	Judgment of 20 December 1974	Dillard	Adversary	joint dissenting opinion	
Nuclear Tests Case (New Zealand v. France)	Judgment of 20 December 1974	Dillard	Adversary	joint dissenting opinion	
Nuclear Tests Case (Australia v. France)/Application by Fiji for permission to intervene	Order of 20 December 1974	Dillard	Adversary		joint declaration
Nuclear Tests Case (New Zealand v. France)/Application by Fiji for permission to intervene	Order of 20 December 1974	Dillard	Adversary		joint declaration
*Western Sahara Case/Request for advisory opinion: request for judge ad hoc	Order of 22 May 1975	Dillard	Advisory		
Western Sahara Case	Advisory Opinion of 16 October 1975	Dillard	Advisory		separate opinion

Aegean Sea Continental Shelf Case (Greece v. Turkey)/Request for the indication of interim measures of protection	Order of 11 September 1976	Dillard	Adversary	X
Aegean Sea Continental Shelf Case/Jurisdiction of the court	Judgment of 19 December 1978	Dillard	Adversary	X
Case Concerning United States Diplomatic and Consular Staff in Tehran (United States of America v. Iran)/Request for the indication of provisional measures	Order of 15 December 1979	Richard R. Baxter	Adversary	X
Case Concerning United States Diplomatic and Consular Staff in Tehran	Judgment of 24 May 1980	Baxter	Adversary	X
**Interpretation of the Agreement of 25 March 1951 between the WHO and Egypt	Advisory Opinion of 20 December 1980	U.S. judge not present	Advisory	
Case Concerning the Continental Shelf (Tunisia/Libyan Arab Jamahiriya/Application by Malta for permission to intervene	Judgment of 14 April 1981	Stephen M. Schwebel	Adversary	separate opinion
Case Concerning Delimitation of the Maritime Boundary in the Gulf of Maine Area (Canada/United States)/Constitution of the chamber	Order of 20 January 1982	Schwebel	Adversary	X

Appendix A (continued)

VOTING RECORD OF U.S. MEMBER OF THE WORLD COURT (1945-85)

CASE/PHASE	JUDGMENT/ORDER	U.S. MEMBER	PROCEEDING	DISSENTED	VOTED WITH MAJORITY
Case Concerning Delimitation of the Maritime Boundary in the Gulf of Maine Area/Composition of the chamber: request for judge ad hoc	Order of 1 February 1982	Schwebel	Adversary		X
Case Concerning the Continental Shelf (Tunisia/Libyan Arab Jamahiriya)	Judgment of 24 February 1982	Schwebel	Adversary		separate opinion
Application for Review of Judgment No. 273 of the United Nations Administrative Tribunal	Advisory Opinion of 20 July 1982	Schwebel	Advisory	X	
Case Concerning the Continental Shelf (Libyan Arab Jamahiriya/Malta/Application by Italy for permission to intervene	Judgment of 21 March 1984	Schwebel	Advisory	X	
Case Concerning Delimitation of the Maritime Boundary in the Gulf of Maine/Appointment of an expert	Order of 30 March 1984	Schwebel	Advisory		X

Case	Date	U.S. Judge	Type		Notes
Case Concerning Military and Paramilitary Activities in and Against Nicaragua (Nicaragua v. United States of America)/Request for the indication of provisional measures	Order of 10 May 1984	Schwebel	Adversary	X	
Case Concerning Military and Paramilitary Activities in and Against Nicaragua/Declaration of intervention of the Republic of El Salvador	Order of 4 October 1984	Schwebel	Adversary	X	
Case Concerning Delimitation of the Maritime Boundary in the Gulf of Maine Area/Composition of the chamber	Judgment of 12 October 1984	Schwebel	Adversary		separate opinion
Case Concerning Military and Paramilitary Activities in and Against Nicaragua/Jurisdiction and admissibility	Judgment of 26 November 1984	Schwebel	Adversary	X	
Case Concerning the Continental Shelf (Libyan Arab Jamahiriya/Malta)	Judgment of 3 June 1985	Schwebel	Adversary	X	

NOTE: Not included in this survey are orders pertaining to time limits for presentation of pleadings—both advisory and adversarial—time extensions, discontinuances, and joinder of claims and parties. Decisions in which there is no indication as to whether the U.S. judge voted with the majority or the dissent owing to an incomplete list of dissenters are excluded from the statistics derived from this chart. These cases are indicated by a single asterisk (*). Also excluded from the statistics derived from this chart are cases decided by the court in which the U.S. judge did not participate. These cases are indicated by a double asterisk (**).

Appendix B

PROPOSED FORM OF QUALIFIED U.S. ACCEPTANCE OF WORLD COURT COMPULSORY JURISDICTION IN ACCORDANCE WITH ARTICLE 36(2) OF THE STATUTE OF THE INTERNATIONAL COURT OF JUSTICE

The government of the United States accepts in conformity with paragraph 2 of article 36 of the Statute of the International Court of Justice, until such time as notice may be given to terminate such acceptance, as compulsory *ipso facto* and without special agreement, and on the basis and condition of reciprocity, the jurisdiction of the International Court of Justice in any dispute, providing that, at the instigation of either party:

(1) a dispute shall be submitted to a chamber of the International Court of Justice consisting of such members of the court as are elected by the court in accordance with the preferences of the parties expressed in an agreement between them, and that, if no such agreement is reached or the court fails to elect the judges named in the agreement, the court shall not be deemed to have jurisdiction over the dispute between those parties;

(2) a dispute shall be submitted to the court, or, at the instance of either party, to an agreed chamber of the court, solely for the purpose of obtaining the determination by the court or its chamber as to the principles and rules of international law applicable to that dispute.

The acceptance of the jurisdiction of the court made by this declaration under paragraph 2 of article 36 of the Statute of the International Court of Justice shall apply to all disputes, subject to the foregoing reservation, other than disputes relating to or connected with facts or situations of hostilities, armed conflicts, individual or collective actions taken in self-defense, resistance to aggression, fulfillment of obligations imposed by international bodies, and other similar or related acts, measures, or situations in which the United States is, has been, or may in the future be, involved.

This acceptance of the jurisdiction of the court shall not apply to disputes in respect of which any other party to the dispute has accepted the compulsory jurisdiction of the International Court of Justice only in relation to or for the purpose of the dispute; or where the acceptance of the court's compulsory jurisdiction on behalf of any other party to the dispute was deposited or ratified less than twelve months prior to the filing of the application bringing the dispute before the court.